# INDO-US RELATIONS
## 1972-91
### A Brief Survey

**Part II**

**Shri Ram Sharma**

2003

DISCOVERY PUBLISHING HOUSE
NEW DELHI-110002

First Published-2003

ISBN 81-7141-662-4



*Published by*

**DISCOVERY PUBLISHING HOUSE**
4831/24, Ansari Road, Prahlad Street,
Darya Ganj, New Delhi-110002 (India)
Phone: 3279245 • Fax: 91-11-3253475
E-mail:dphtemp@indiatimes.com

***Printed at:***
**Arora Offset Press**
**Laxmi Nagar, Delhi 110 092.**

**To**

**Professor Jaidev Mohanlal Dave**

eminent scientist and a teacher par excellence with
profound gratitude of young scientists of
Ram's generation charged with the mission
to make our society science-minded

# Preface

The idea of bringing out a set of small monographs on the major world events in which India got involved since independence was mooted at a small ad hoc group of teachers who shared one common experience among themselves namely that the lack of small and dependable publications on Indian foreign policy was the main handicap which the undergraduates in state universities had to put up with while pursuing the scope of the syllabus they were supposed to go through. There was no dearth of lengthy treatises on all those subjects that in one way or the other, fell under the purview of Indian foreign policy, and on how the various issues emerged and how, some of them developed into crises to tackle which India had to adopt a certain line of action.

Then there was emerging a new generation of young political activists who for their own public relations activities felt impelled to look for such publications as would provide them, for ready reference, with information about what role India has been playing in various spheres of world politics to safeguard its national interests. Of late a happy trend in public thinking has demonstrated that the people no longer keep their interests confined to domestic issues but go on trying to seek information on various world events which have their inescapable impact on our national politics. In almost all public addresses eminent politicians have to make important policy statements to keep the people informed of what has been going on in the sphere of world politics. In regional press the comments on world issues have assumed much significance. It is to cater to the intellectual interests of these two major segments of readership that this project has been taken in hand. The readers' response to the previous publications has further justified the inception of this venture.

To begin with, priority has been given to India's relations with the three major powers, USA, USSR and China as thereby most of the world events related to India's interests are easily covered. There has hardly been any problem of international significance which in one way or the other was not affected by the policies of either of these powers. It is through influencing the policies of these powers that India sought to achieve some of the major goals of its foreign policy.

The preparation of this monograph has been solely based on the published material in the form of books and periodicals and, above all, press comments in our national dailies as well as some foreign newspapers. A very comprehensive work in two volumes on this period of India's foreign policy has been completed by Professor M.S. Rajan in collaboration with his devoted colleagues but for reasons which have remained unknown, it remains unpublished. Thus its inaccessibility to general readership has deprived many of us of the benefit we could draw from the valuable information contained there in.

The three chapters in the second volume, each dealing with India's relations with USA, USSR and China have been contributed by Professor P. Sahdevan. The author received with gratitude much guidance from the pattern followed in these chapters and also regarding the information of events that determined the course of relations between India and the super powers during the period under survey. In procuring material from the ICSSR sources, Dr. Suresh Chander has been of great help to me for which he deserves all credit and appreciation.

**S.R. Sharma**

# Contents

*Preface*

1. Introduction 1
2. Bangladesh Crisis: Aftermath 9
3. Towards Reconciliation 13
4. Janata Regime 28
5. The Afghan Crisis 43
6. Indira Gandhi's Come back 54
7. Rajiv Gandhi in Office 70
8. The Pakistan Factor 86
9. Defence Cooperation 99
10. The Nuclear Factor 109
11. Economic and Scientific Interactions 118
12. The Miscellany 132
13. Concluding Observations 144

*Index* 153

# 1

# Introduction

During the period under survey Indo-US relations were not marked by any consistency; they fluctuated from time to time on the nature of issues involved and the manner in which the parties in power meant to tackle them. American policies are not determined by the likes and dislikes of the occupants in White House; they are subject to the information provided by the administration. The policies are usually hatched in the bureaucratic set up which is well equipped with all sorts of information concerning world affairs. The political chief, the US President, has to act in most cases, as their spokesman. On personal level, there may be amity and goodwill as it was between Morarji Desai and President Carter but when it came to the nuclear issue, the latter could be as tough and blunt as his predecessors Nixon and Reagan. Again in dealing with relations between India and Pakistan, even the most well disposed President Kennedy had to admit that he was on the horns of dilemma, it was a choice of appeasing an ally and damaging the friendship of a big power.

Moreover, the professions of friendship voiced by the politicians do not mean much to those who know what motivates the expression of their goodwill. As an illustration one has to recall how solicitous President Carter was when he enquired twice on the phone, about the state of health of Jay Prakash Narayan who was then in his sickbed in a nursing home at Seattle ignoring the fact that at that very moment the US administration was handing over two naval destroyers to Pakistan.[1]

It was a kind of replay of what had happened during the Bangladesh crisis in 1971 when Swaran Singh External Affairs Minister, went to Washington to plead with the Nixon administration to do something to relieve India of the tension caused by the influx of over 9 million refugees from the then East Pakistan. After expressing sympathy with India's plight and assuring liberal economic aid for the upkeep of the refugees, the US leadership suggested that a joint statement be issued in which the Indian guest would state his satisfaction with the outcome of talks. Swaran Singh refused to do that on the obvious ground that the refugee problem was an offshoot of the ruthless suppression committed by the Pakistan army with the arms supplied to them by the USA. The day Swaran Singh left, the *New York Times* reported that a new bulk of the US arms was being loaded in a freighter bound for Pakistan.[2]

It has often been repeated that India and the US shared democratic values and as such they had every reason to be close to each other. But it has been a painful experience that almost in all important issues in which India was involved, American sympathies were in favour of its adversaries. Some of these crises were, Kashmir in 1947 and 1965, Goa in 1961 and Bangladesh in 1971. India fought for the protection of democratic values but in every case, the US backed those like Pakistan and Portugal when both of them were under the iron-heel of dictatorship.

Indo-US relations fell into two phases, one may be called positive phase when we talked about our cultural ties, democratic traditions, economic and scientific cooperation and the rest of it. In these matters there were more positive efforts to seek constructive cooperation which was forthcoming from each side. The other one was the irritant phase which included many more issues that caused clash between our national interests and American strategic considerations. Specifically they were, arms aid to Pakistan, discriminatory approach to India's aspiration to use nuclear energy for peaceful purposes, insistence on our signing the NPT, building bases in Indian Ocean and, above all, reservations about India's efforts to improve relations with China and the Soviet Union.

Despite the fact that there had been no direct conflict of interest between these two countries, they continued to differ over their relations with third countries like China, the Soviet Union, Vietnam and mainly Pakistan. Differences arose on the principle of approach towards other countries in the developments of which each country felt involved. In view of the futility of such negative approach, both sides had started realising that before there could be any meaningful improvement in Indo-US relations each side would have to shed some of the basic assumptions which made them view each other's activities with suspicion.

Equally important was the psychological factor which impeded the development of mature relationship between the two countries. The US considered itself a paragon of democratic system which others should regard as a model to be emulated. India was irrevocably committed to develop its own style of democracy in the light of what its cultural, political and economic background demanded of it. Americans judged our working system with values that were not generally applied by them in their dealings with other countries with different political systems. The American liberals felt assured of India's day to day performance as practical manifestation of the democratic spirit which urged the government to undertake the economic reforms to meet their periodic requirements. The conservatives, on the other hand, tended to take the diametrically opposed view that the democratic values could be sustained only through a matching tradition of economic liberalism that guaranteed private enterprise its due place in its socio-economic system.

If at times, the US administration had been sensitive to what were reasonable aspirations of Indian people, the reason was that the Americans believed as a matter of conviction that India was a power of the future. It could not be a match to China in claiming to have achieved equal measure of progress in the economic field but the democratic system that it applied to seek to solve its national problems stood the test of time. If economic aid was liberally extended by other democratic countries with absolutely altruistic motives, it could emerge in the next decade as a major global power.[3]

In the wake of Bangladesh crisis, efforts were seriously initiated by the US administration to mollify the hurt sentiments of Indian people. To start with, Kissinger's visit in the last week of October 1974 was the first step in that direction. Kissinger on his arrival, stated that his visit was intended to renew the longstanding friendship, remove old misunderstandings and build a new mature relationship between the two countries. He also announced the extension of the US food assistance to India but without mentioning any figure. Regarding allegations against CIA, he said Washington would take strongest action against any American official agency indulging in undesirable activities. On the crucial issue of arms supplies to Pakistan he merely stated that the US would not take any step that would promote arms race in the subcontinent. But he refused to elaborate his statement in specific terms as any thing spoken on the Indian soil would evoke adverse reaction in Pakistan.

Indo-US relations which remained strained since the Bangladesh crisis were further affected by the indiscreet act of Mrs. Gandhi in declaring the emergency in June 1975. The US administration continued to watch the developments in India during the emergency period and tried to see how pressure could be brought about to bear on her to undo that wrong. The US did not consider it to be its exclusive concern to bring about the restoration of normal state of civic affairs in India but sought the cooperation of other democratic countries of Western Europe to exert their influence on Mrs. Gandhi to end the emergency. The US spokesman often made some comments which were not received well in the official quarters in India. Gradually Mrs. Gandhi's view point also came to be regarded as somewhat valid for the oppressive steps she had taken at the cost of civil liberties. However, a sort of tension continued to mark the relations between the two countries till March 1977 when the new Janata party came to power.

President Carter's visit in January 1978, was in a way, in continuation of the confidence building measures adopted by his predecessors as it was a consensus in American official public opinion that in their own interests India could not be taken lightly. In the new Prime Minister, Morarji Desai, he found a soul mate with whom he could talk on the same wavelength though there could be some notes of dissent on what they sought to communicate to each other on issues of common interests. During the talks Carter could not avoid talking about Indo-Pak and Indo-Soviet relations as these were the issues on which each side had to understand the other's view point.

As regards Indo-Pak relations, Carter realised the force in Indian argument that the two Asian neighbours could not come closer until the US ceased to give arms aid including the nuclear support to Pakistan. In this context, the nuclear issue was discussed in detail as a result of which Carter felt convinced that so long as Morarji was in power, India would not use nuclear energy for war purposes. Likewise, American allegations regarding India's tilt towards Soviet Union were found to be not very relevant in the context of new developments in India. Carter took no time to realise that Morarji was true in his professions to follow a balanced policy towards the two super powers. The Carter visit in brief turned out to be a conciliatory gesture with which the leadership of both the countries felt reassured.

A perceptible change was witnessed, after Morarji Desai's visit to the USA in the style of carrying on negotiations on different issues of common interest to both the countries. Differences were handled not with acrimony but with the guiding motive to understand each other's compulsions, both domestic as well as international, in adopting a particular line of thinking. The termination of refuelling facilities for the US aircraft during the Gulf war was a particularly awkward episode, but the US appreciated the fact that India with its policy of non-alignment and a big muslim population was under severe compulsions to take that decision.[4]

Afghanistan remained for long an unresolved issue among the three major powers, USA, USSR and China. They realised the futility of prolonging this conflict. By 1986 the three agreed to treat it as a major irritant. This led to the conclusion of the April 1988 accord on Afghanistan to which Pakistan, Afghanistan, the Soviet Union and the USA were the signatory powers. China was not a direct participant in the negotiations but China was an important factor in the decision making process of the accord. China supported the US and quietly persuaded Pakistan to sign it. The Soviet forces started withdrawing from February 1989.

During the Afghanistan crisis Indian grievance was that the Indian proposal in favour of a political solution as against the Western action in opposing the Soviet intervention by a huge influx of arms through Pakistan was ignored by the US and its allies. India was given less credit than it deserved for how consistently it continued to urge the Soviet Union to reach an honourable settlement with the USA on this issue. It was also not well understood that India was not less concerned than others with the Soviet intervention in Afghanistan as it had indirectly threatened India's own security. It was in the name of Soviet intervention that Pakistan was being armed by American weapons which had little use in Afghanistan but which could be used against India.[5]

Major hurdle in the process of achieving a negotiated settlement was that while Moscow expected an independent Afghan government with a pro-Soviet policy, Washington covertly sought to instal a pro-American government in Afghanistan. Indian view was that the decision about the type of government be left to the Afghan people themselves as it was an internal matter for them. The immediate task was to restore normalcy the first step towards which would be the withdrawal of troops.

After the collapse of the Soviet Union, the US remained the most powerful state capable of exercising global hegemony. Moreover, the American victory in the Gulf war further raised its status as a power which would have its say in a crisis in which it was forced to get involved. Indian leadership was clearly given to understand that Russia remained in constant touch with what was going on in the Gulf war, how it broke out and why America intervened in it. Moscow was also assured that the majority of the countries including most of the Arab world supported the American move. The Gulf war and the events following it had shown that the USA could only lead in cooperation with other powers, not by the unilateral exercise of its power. New Delhi realised that the allegation of charging the US as playing the role of a world policeman was not very rational. It would therefore not be difficult for India in doing business with such a strengthened America not only on economic issues but also on other subjects of wider significance.

The US had expected a change in India's foreign policy approach in their favour and therefore, an improvement in Indo-US relations any time there had been a change of prime minister in this country. They entertained such hopes when Shastri succeeded Nehru in 1964, when Mrs. Gandhi succeeded Shastri in 1966 and when Morarji displaced Mrs. Gandhi in 1977. After Rajiv Gandhi's death in 1991, it was felt in some American political circles that there might be some coolness in Indo-US relations. A confidential Congress report held a different view. It stated that the political leaders of the day seemed to have a realistic view of India's interactions with the US and the international community including multilateral lending institutions such as the IMF and the World Bank. Consequently, India's financial problems would constrain its options and may cause India's leaders to seek better ties with the US and other industrialised countries like Germany and Japan.[6] The report acknowledged that the Indo-US ties could be damaged if political instability would lead to more human rights abuses in Punjab and Kashmir. But if Indian government's efforts to accommodate the regional dissidents in the larger constitutional framework succeeded there would be more sympathy and support for India in the US.

The report noted that during the Gulf war, Chandra Sekhara government tilted India's policy towards anti-Iraq alliance and allowed US transport air-crafts to refuel at Bombay enroute to the Gulf. This policy continued until Rajiv Gandhi intervened and threatened to withdraw support from the Chandra Shekhar government. Later this happened on a different political issue. The government was accused of ordering Haryana police to spy on Rajiv.[7] It had nothing to do with the step Chandra Shekhar took in regard to refuelling facility provided to the US air crafts going to the war theatre.

## REFERENCES

1. C. Raghavan in the *Mainstream* 28 May 1977, p. 5-6
2. Ibid
3. Bhabani Sen Gupta in *Hindustan Times* 11 October 1991
4. Ambassador Abid Hussain's statement in *Times of India* 8 August 1991 reported by T.K.. Menon from Washington
5. Prof. M.S. Rajan, *India's Foreign Relations* (MSS) Vol. I., p. 450
6. Aziz Haniffa in *Hindustan Times* 1 June 1991
7. Ibid

# 2

# Bangladesh Crisis: Aftermath

The Bangladesh war in which the two countries took opposite sides created a sense of alienation between India and the US. India's grievance has been that the American leadership did not view the Bangladesh crisis in correct perspective. What was lamentable was that the century old American civil war rhetoric against secession was still strong in the American memory. Americans who have been in the vanguard in advocating the independence of colonial regimes in Asia did not automatically recognise that the independence of the people of East Pakistan was also an issue of self-determination.[1] The result was that the American administration continued to make vain efforts to convince the world that what was happening in East Bengal was nothing but a secessionist movement which should be treated as such. But such an argument cut little ice with those whom they wanted to impress with their version of crisis. More than that, some of their puerile statements made them look ridiculous.

When on 16 December 1971, India announced ceasefire, Kissinger took it to be a reluctant decision resulting from Soviet pressure which in turn, grew out of American initiative including the seventh fleet movement.[2] This statement was later contradicted by his deputy Christopher Hollen who said that Kissinger was wrong in concluding that Nixon's willingness to risk war with the Soviet Union, including the deployment of a US aircraft carrier to South Asia saved West Pakistan and preserved the structure of peace.[3]

Kissinger, however, believed that Nixon somehow felt convinced that India was out to destroy West Pakistan and this he was determined not to allow to happen. To achieve this he said he had to arrange a series of secret meetings with ambassador Huang Hua of China to coordinate their policies, in thwarting India's plans. He had also sent stern messages to Moscow to pressure India not to go ahead with its designs against West Pakistan. To cap it all he had to order an air craft carrier task force to proceed through the straits of Malacca into Bay of Bengal to back up his warning with a show of force.[4]

These statements seemed to be quite strange in view of how Mrs. Gandhi and his advisers tried to read the developments taking place during the Bangladesh crisis at the initiative of the US. They believed that the seventh fleet business in the Indian Ocean was a symbolic gesture meant for consumption by Pakistan, China and the muslim states of West Asia. Moreover, the US was not going to take up cudgels on behalf of Pakistan when it was bogged down in Vietnam. Besides, the fleet was under consistent Soviet surveillance and the Government of India was kept informed about its movements. In any case Dacca was expected to fall before the fleet could do any thing about it.[5]

What annoyed Indian leadership most was the statement President Nixon made taking credit for India's decision to ceasefire on the western front after the fall of Dacca. Mrs. Gandhi considered it one of the most perverse statements that came out of the White House on Bangladesh crisis. Equally absurd was the statement that India wanted to 'gobble up' West Pakistan. If India had some design on West Pakistan, Mrs. Gandhi said, she would not have ordered unilateral ceasefire and invited Bhutto to discuss the matter with her.[6] Quite understandably, even Pakistan believed the American version. Bhutto was reported to have said that if the US had not given a firm warning that the hostilities must cease, India could not have halted the war. He further recalled that when he had been to Peking a little after the crisis was over, Chou En-lai had also confirmed that the US had put its foot down.[7]

Public reactions at home and abroad were so critical over those indiscreet utterances of some of the American leaders that the official spokesmen often felt embarrassed as it caused avoidable tension in Indo-US relations and annoyance among the south and south eastern countries most of which viewed the Bangladesh crisis as a historic struggle for liberation of an ethnic nationality against the domination of a powerful group. Another consequence of this shortsighted policy of the US was the enhancement of Soviet prestige in this region much to the disadvantage of the US. Even in their own calculation the Sino-US rapprochement reached during the crisis was not of much avail to either of them as the aims and motives which led them to a compromise were extremely at variance with each other.

In the immediate post-crisis period, the US stood resolutely opposed to India for the latter's role in Bangladesh crisis. What added to their annoyance was that all it happened despite the Sino-US rapprochement which, in their view, would have caused some punitive effect on India. Both wanted to stall the liberation developments to retain status quo in Bangladesh. But neither of them, despite its power consciousness and capacity for strategic manipulations could succeed in rolling back the tide of Bangladesh nationalism. It was apprehended in India that the new found friendship between Peking and Washington may continue to stir up trouble in other ways.

Another fact to be kept in view is that with the break up of the two wings of Pakistan, India acquired a new status in South Asia. It was assumed in some diplomatic circles that India, out of overconfidence, may dictate terms to Pakistan and have its will prevail over some issues which had to be settled in the post crisis period. If India acted that way, China and the US would continue to remain united to oppose any such move on the part of India.

Neither of these two contingencies could occur partly because India was fully satisfied by its achievement, and had no mind to clamour for any more gains and partly because both China and the US had gradually getting reconciled to the inevitability of the event and treat Bangladesh as a fait accompli which they could not undo. Now there was no option to them but to come to terms with India. Indian leaders admitted that the newly acquired position gave them a great advantage but it had also cast upon them a certain responsibility. The US President in his message to the Congress had definitely committed his country not to join any grouping or pursue any policy against India.[8].

## REFERENCES

1. Max Lerner in *Tribune,* 4 March 1971. For a very informative article, see M..S. Rajan, Bangladesh and After, *Pacific Affairs*, Vol. 26, No. 2, Summer 1972.
2. P.N. Dhar, *Indira Gandhi, the Emergency and Indian Democracy*, p. 182.
3. Ibid., p. 180
4. Ibid.
5. Shashi Tharoor, *Reasons of State: Political Developments in Indian Foreign Policy under Mrs. Indira Gandhi 1966-77*, p. 17.
6. *New York Times*, 13 February 1972.
7. *Foreign Affairs Record*, Vol. 18 (1972), p. 90.
8. *Department of State Bulletin no. 1749*, 4 June 1973, p. 792 cited in P. Sahadevan p. 652.

# 3

# Towards Reconciliation

It may be recalled that on 15 December 1971 Mrs. Gandhi wrote to Nixon on Bangladesh crisis taking strong exception to the American insinuations and innuendoes that it was India which precipitated the crisis and thwarted the emergence of a solution. Nixon in his brief reply said that he did not agree with Mrs. Gandhi's version and promised a fuller reply in due course. Though the response remained unintimated, it was clearly spelt out in the message that Nixon sent to the Congress in February 1972.

He assured the Congress that the political as well as economic relationship with India would naturally be subject to dialogue between the two countries. The US would have the continuing interest in India's independence and nonalignment and if India maintained balanced relationship with the major powers, the US would respond constructively. The statement by implication clearly meant that if in dealing with the super powers India's policy was not tilted towards the Soviet Union, the US would respond constructively to the requirements of India, one of which was for foodgrains. Of greater interest to Nixon was that India behaved with Pakistan with generosity.[1]

In the post-crisis phase American attitude began to evolve towards being more rational. It was evident from the statement made by an official spokesman, Herbert Klaein who was authorised to say that the disagreements caused during the Bangladesh crisis would not make the administration 'anti-India' any more. In his view whatever misunderstanding arose during the crisis was due to lack of understanding of each other's viewpoint; it was a passing phase which was over with the emergence of Bangladesh as a sovereign state.[2] In accordance with his assurance, Nixon sent on 5 July 1972 his special envoy John B. Connolly to New Delhi where he met Mrs. Gandhi and other leaders in his efforts to make it clear to them on how the US administration was viewing the post-crisis phase problems between the two countries.[3]

The visit of Connolly was not expected to achieve any spectacular result; it was solely meant to set in motion the process of improving Indo-US relations. The damage caused during the crisis period was too severe to be healed by one visit. Nixon wanted to know how the Indian leadership would respond to such a friendly gesture. Indian leadership was not lacking in giving a suitable response which was provided by Mrs. Gandhi's statement that if the US was genuinely anxious to be friends, we would welcome it. This signalled the commencement of a new phase in Indo-US relations in which both the parties felt inclined to bury the unpleasant past and start afresh on a new note of cordiality.

Three other events helped in the process of normalisation of relations between the two countries. One was the withdrawal of Indian forces to a man from the territory of Bangladesh which they had won from Pakistani hands. This was followed by the repatriation of Pak prisoners of war to their country. Secondly new government in Bangladesh was generous enough to accede to India's suggestion to abandon their claim to try some Pak Generals for war crimes. Finally, the signing of the Simla pact together by Mrs. Gandhi and Z.A. Bhutto to normalise Indo-Pak relations which would mean observance of the line of actual control, cessation of hostile propaganda in each country against the other and restoration of diplomatic relations between the two countries contributed considerably in appeasing the sentiments of the American leadership.

With the gradual disappearance of these irritants the US administration was in a chastened mood and willing to let-by gone be by gone. Nixon's birthday message to Mrs. Gandhi on 19 November 1972 was not a mere diplomatic courtesy. He had expressed the hope that the two countries could develop a sounder relationship based on understanding and respect for mutual interests.

Further a decision taken by the US administration in 1973 also helped in restoring confidence in Indian mind about the US bonafides in improving their relations with India. It was related to the release of $87.6 million development aid for India which remained suspended since December 1971.[4] Although the official spokesman maintained that the decision to this effect was unrelated to the US administration's announcement of lifting the embargo on military supplies to Pakistan the timing of Washington's decision indicated that it was intended to mollify the Indian resentment on US arms supplies to Pakistan. A similar agreement was signed in the same year (1973) regarding the settlement of the surplus accumulation arising from the PL 480 wheat sales to India. These two minor acts of generosity on the part of the US further cleared the way towards reconciliation between the two countries.[5]

To appease the Indian sentiments Kissinger reiterated what the US administration had earlier held out; the US would not engage in a massive supply of arms to Pakistan to trigger off arms race in South Asia and it would not deliver arms to the extent that would affect the underlying strategic balance. This sort of assurance did not cut much ice with the Indians.[6] A queer logic that India could not understand was that the US warned India to delink the issue of arms supply from the overall process of improving Indo-US relations. They could continue to supply arms to Pakistan which would be used against India but Indians should not mind this inimical act and continue to smile at the US in the hope that some patronage would be extended to them.[7]

There was another issue; the growing US-Soviet detente in the wake of Nixon-Brezhnev summit which Kissinger sought to clear what this development actually meant. He said it should not cause concern in third world countries because it was not an exercise aimed at carving out spheres of influence or deciding the fate of other countries behind their back. What these two super powers sought to do was to import something like the 'Simla spirit' into their own relations.[8] Kissinger asked if old adversaries like India and Pakistan could engage in efforts to reconcile their differences, why could they USA and USSR not do the same?

In view of these conciliatory statements, Indian government felt a little softened and opportunities were utilised to respond to them concretely even on personal level. When Mrs. Gandhi was on official visit to Canada in June 1973, she visited Niagra falls which formed the US-Canada boundary. She also decided to visit Lake Placid which was in New York state for a brief meeting with her old teacher Mrs. Kyle. It was a private visit but the US ambassador in India Moynhin was there at President Nixon's instance to look after Mrs. Gandhi's comforts while she was on the American territory.[9]

The change of leadership in the US took place in August 1974 when President Nixon was found guilty of involvement in the Watergate scandal. He was succeeded by Gerald Ford who was the Vice-president during the days of Nixon. In India it was regarded as a hopeful event as Nixon was recalled as one who had contributed a great deal to the deterioration of Indo-US relations by being too pro-Pakistani in his dealings with India. Mrs. Gandhi, in particular had developed a personal distrust and animus for him. She somehow had come to believe that Nixon had tried several times to overthrow her government through covert activities of the CIA. During Nixon's time foreign policy discussions between the two countries were left to be conducted by the External Affairs Minister and the US Secretary of State.

President Ford on assuming office made several overtures to India. He assured Swaran Singh, External Affairs Minister on 20 September 1974 at the White House that he would do his best to improve and strengthen the Indo-US relations.[10] This was a good beginning but the subsequent events revealed that the relations between the two countries were not going to be as smooth as expected. India was keen to see that the US actually behaved in a friendly fashion as it was in need of assistance to overcome the food shortage which was acute at that time. The US, on the other hand, was more interested in arming Pakistan to be a match to India.

India's nuclear explosion in May 1974 did not evoke much adverse comments from the American side partly because it was viewed as a primitive device which could not lead to some serious consequences and partly because it was viewed as a small attempt in reaction to the Chinese bomb blasted a decade ago. A section of the elite would have been happy if India could come out with a suitable response to the Chinese challenge. However, the official response was one of mild annoyance at India having crossed the nuclear Rubicon. This was expressed in the US Congress decision to delete a $ 25 million development loan to India recommended by the Nixon administration in its foreign aid bill. But curiously enough the US State Department argued against linking the country's aid policy with India's nuclear test. More important was the Nixon administration's reported reaffirmation that it would not change its arms supply policy towards India and Pakistan following the Indian blast.[11] India felt assured that now the US would not withhold the aid for wrong reasons as it would lead to undesirable consequences.

**Merger of Sikkim**

On this issue the official reaction was quite moderate regarding it as an 'internal matter' quite within the constitutional framework of the Indo-Sikkim treaty of 1960.[12] The US view was further modified by an external factor namely China's proximity to this region and its consistent efforts to create border troubles. Now with the total merger of the State to the Indian Union it would become an integral part of the country and expand its influence over to the other side of the border where the Chinese forces stood face to face with Indian troops.

In some non-official circles, the reactions were very severely critical. India was blamed for practising colonialism which it criticised when practised by the western world. Mrs. Gandhi was particularly held responsible for practising a highly selective sort of morality that held the violation of nationhood a vicious evil. It was an exception when she practised it herself on a prey that was weak and small.[13]

In the US Senate, Clairborne Pell contended that twice before, in the case of Goa and in its conflict with Pakistan on the Bangladesh issue, India had used military force in an effort to alter the map of South Asia. He could not think of any other nation since World War II that could match Indian government's record of forceful expansion of its territories. Another Senator denounced India's blatant 'aggression' which paralleled Anschluss of Austria in 1938 and Soviet action in Czechoslovakia in 1968.[14]

**Kissinger's Visit**

Henry Kissinger, the US Secretary of State was in India for three days from 27 to 30 October 1974 on a friendly mission to renew long-standing friendship, remove all misunderstandings and build a new relationship between the two countries. Before leaving for India, Kissinger made the confession that the US 'tilt' against India which was last demonstrated in 1971 was over and the balance had been restored. During his talks he characterised his visit as marking a 'new phase', and providing a good base for 'mature' Indo-US relationship. He did not make any claim for his country beyond saying that it believed in the worth of India's friendship. What was significant, more than once during his visit, he readily agreed to extend recognition to India as a 'major power' and during his press conference at the end of his visit he went so far as to equate India with America as being two major powers.[15]

Kissinger was careful to point out that the Indian government did not need apprehend that Sino-US rapprochement would in any way affect Indo-US relations. The US being a democracy was quite understandably much nearer to a democracy such as India. The US also had to deal with dictatorships like the USSR because the latter possessed the capability to cause a nuclear holocaust. Similarly it was not possible to have a peaceful international environment without regular contacts with countries like China but that did not mean approbation of the domestic structure of the government there.[16]

He made it clear that the US did not consider the Indo-Soviet treaty and the way it was being implemented as something detrimental to the American interests in the region, since the US was satisfied that India was following its own foreign policy in pursuit of its larger national interests.[17] On the crucial issue of the US resuming arms supply to Pakistan, Kissinger merely repeated what his administration had earlier assured namely that Washington would not take any step that would provoke arms race in the sub continent. He refused to say more on this issue as it was likely to affect the US-Pak relations. It clearly implied to India that the US was still thinking in terms of equating India with Pakistan.

On the nuclear question he was assured that India's policy was not to allow development of nuclear weapons as it was pledged to use nuclear energy for peaceful purposes. This assurance was meant to pacify Pakistan and help the US administration to defuse the misguided propaganda that India was ignoring the economic development projects giving priority to developing nuclear capability. He was also told that whatever nuclear aid India had offered to non-nuclear states was given solely with the object that it would be used only for constructive uses.[18] He welcomed India's nuclear policy not to embark on a weapon programme. He said that the US would consult India about the safeguards which it considered useful and which it was prepared to apply to itself in preventing nuclear proliferation.

These were some of the innocuous issues on which Kissinger could give his clarification by way of assurance to India. But during his visit he gave no assurance of the embargo on arms supply to Pakistan nor, more important, did he say anything encouraging about Diego Garcia which his administration was developing into a major base in the Indian Ocean. Subsequent events disclosed that the so called tilt continued with more American arms assured to Pakistan and Diego Garcia was being developed to counter the security threat to the small littoral states. Above all, the fact that he could not mobilise India for a common front against the OPEC despite the difficulties that we had to face because of the oil price hike, clearly suggested that we had to act in defence of our national interests which, in this case, meant our solidarity with the oil producing Arab States.[19]

What was the net result of Kissinger's visit? His visit was intended to correct the 'Nixon tilt' towards Pakistan with a view to making Indo-US relations a little relaxed. But the trend of talks revealed that even this little objective was not achieved as Kissinger neither admitted the error of US administration in being so unreasonably hostile to India during the Bangladesh crisis which, in all fairness Washington was morally bound to support, nor did he make any proposal which would have effaced some of the bitter memories of the frustrating meeting Mrs. Gandhi had with Nixon on the eve of Bangladesh crisis.

In actual terms, the contribution of Kissinger's visit to the improvement of Indo-US relations was minimal. The relations remained cool and distant; personal contacts between the top leaderships of the two countries remained a remote possibility and even the official correspondence was marked by expressions of apathy and indifference. The exit of Nixon due to Watergate scandal, and his succession by Ford gave some hope for a new turn in Indo-US relations. Mrs. Gandhi welcomed his assuming office with hope and confidence but Kissinger continued as the Secretary of State to direct the course of US foreign policy relations. On 24 July 1975, the Ford administration announced its decision to completely lift the embargo, imposed in 1965, on the supply of arms and military equipment to Pakistan. This was reported to have been done to appease the Pakistani Prime Minister Bhutto who was in Washington in the first week of February 1975. To US government this step was both 'necessary' and 'logical' in view of its policy to create 'stability' among its friends and 'to take steps to maintain their security'.

In view of these developments the decision to set up a joint business council to increase direct contacts between business sectors of the two countries and the US government's willingness to sell one million tons of wheat worth $170 million to India did not create any perceptive impact on Indo-American relations.[20] The US also assured that it had no intention to resume its pre-1965 policy which sought to equate Pakistan with India through the input of US arms nor was it now about to engage in an open-ended policy of granting Pakistan every thing it required. Such an assurance had no meaning to India. The External Affairs Minister Y.B. Chavan who was to go to Washington to attend a meeting of the Indo-US joint commission postponed his visit for an indefinite period. Probably in retaliation Kissinger asked William Saxbe the US ambassador designate to postpone his trip by a week. He later arrived here on 8 March 1975. It was also speculated that President Ford may be advised to call off his proposed visit to India in 1975. Such pinpricks went on intermittently till June 1975 when the declaration of the emergency made the matters worse.

### Proclamation of the Emergency

While the negotiations were going on, on how to ease tension caused in the relations of the two countries by the resumption of American arms supply to Pakistan, came the news that the Government of India had declared the 'emergency' on 27 June 1975. On 17 September, President Ford in a press interview said that it was very sad that 600 million people had lost what they had since the mid-forties but he hoped that in short time there would be a restoration of democratic process as they knew it in their country.[21]

Having known the high-handedness with which Mrs. Gandhi tried to impose the conditions of the emergency resulting in the arbitrary arrests and imprisonments of her political rivals, denial of fundamental freedoms and even curtailment of some of the privileges of Parliament, President Ford called off his proposed visit to India which was going to take place later in the year. His administration also liberally extended political asylum to a number of leading political leaders. The official view apart, even those who were friendly towards India were not happy with the undemocratic step which Mrs. Gandhi had taken. India, in their view had always been regarded as the strongest bastion of democracy in Asia and the impact of emergency amounted to a let down. There was another problem. In the new foreign aid bill that was going to be introduced in the Congress, a provision was going to be included to the effect that the aid would be denied to those countries who would condone such practice as prolonged detention without trial.[22]

President Ford's comments evoked strong feelings among the Indian people. Every society takes measures to protect its stability and ideals, India no less than the United States. The foreign office spokesman observed that it was amazing that the US President had chosen to comment on the internal affairs of a friendly country without due appreciation of the issues involved. The Indian people were committed to democracy as enshrined in their constitutions; and the measures taken were provided in the constitution. Indian side scrupulously avoided making any comments on several aspects of the internal policies of the US like the situation of civil liberties and the extra ordinary powers exercised by the executive in certain circumstances. It is because the accepted norms of international relations did not permit official comments from outside.[23]

Mrs. Gandhi added her voice to such outcries. She did not openly refer to the cancellation of President Ford's visit to India but she was quite scathing in her criticism of those countries that had assumed upon themselves the responsibility of intervening in the internal affairs of other countries by military means as well as by economic pressure. She was sorry to observe that different standards had been applied by the western media in dealing with Indian affairs. She also said that official visits by the heads of state of the democratic countries were being paid to countries, like China where not a semblance of democracy was perceptible in their working of the government but, on the other hand, whatever little happened in India was not acceptable to them. However, the comment made was ill-timed. It renewed friction between the two countries at a time when hopes had been revived of establishing cordiality in their relations. After much efforts Indo-US joint commission had been renewed and its first meeting was scheduled in Washington on 6 October which Y.B. Chavan was going to attend. Such statements were likely to damage the prospects of confidence building moves sponsored by both sides.

Realising the possibility of the emergency to continue for an indefinite period, any adverse comments by the American leaders would further cause estrangement in the relations of the two countries, the government as well as the non-governmental agencies started feeling reconciled to what was happening in India. Moreover, they also tried to see the plus points of the emergency period which could not be viewed from a partisan point of view.

During the emergency not only a certain section of media but also some government agencies praised the economic progress achieved by India during the emergency. The journal *Commerce India*, published by the US Department of Commerce dated 2 August 1975 highlighted through the graphs the growing two-way trade between India and the USA. The journal said that India had survived its most difficult crisis since independence and a remarkable turn about had occurred in the Indian economy during the past year. Industrial production increased by 4.5 per cent in 1976 and improvement in the balance of payments position permitted the government to import raw material, and equipment for further developments in the country. The journal concluded that the governments policy towards foreign investment was selective but there was attraction for American firms to invest in India.[24]

On the government level Kissinger was reported to have given clear instructions to his officers not to make any comments on what was India's internal matter. Subsequently as an unusual gesture Mrs. Gandhi attended one of the American ambassador, Saxbe's dinner. Further, India's representative at the UN was asked not to insist on including the issue of Porte Rico in the UN General Assembly agenda as it would cause embarrassment to US.

Later, Ford during the visit of Y.B. Chavan, External Affairs Minister, told him that he meant no offence by his earlier statement about the enforcement of the emergency in India. The President further assured him that his proposed visit to India was not cancelled, it was merely postponed to some convenient date. The State Department in a subsequent clarification said that no actual date for the President's visit was fixed, so the question of postponement did not arise. As regards the President's comments, they merely underlined the traditional American preference for democratic political system. The Indian reactions were based on misunderstanding.

The general impression in some American political circles was that during the emergency Mrs. Gandhi followed an out and out pro-Soviet policy. It was in return to the support extended by the Soviet government to the measures she had adopted to tone up the administration. But she was also anxious to improve relations with the USA. In other words the policy she followed was to narrow the gap between India's warmth for the Soviet Union and indifference towards the USA.

Within a couple of days after proclaiming emergency Mrs. Gandhi in a national broadcast on 27 June declared that the government had no plans to nationalise industries or impose any new controls. She said this to refute the rumours that were set afloat following the imposition of emergency. To further support Mrs. Gandhi's statement the President,

Fakhruddin Ali Ahmad on 23 April 1976 inaugurating the session of the Associated Chamber of Commerce encouraged the private sector to demonstrate its willingness and capacity to contribute its due share to the country's economic development.

As the subsequent events suggested, the President's call was well received by the private sector to improve the climate of investment. Approval of capital issues granted by the government to non-government companies during 1975-76 amounted to Rs. 293.94 crores as against Rs. 198.90 crores during the previous year. The paid up capital raised by those companies increased to Rs. 169.60 crores during 1975-76 from Rs. 162.22 crores in the previous year. The government wanted that the private sector should take full advantage of the new incentives that the government had offered.[25]

Mrs. Gandhi, on her part, made every effort to refute whatever anti-American statements were made by the opposition. For instance, when they took exception to President Ford's statement criticising the imposition of the emergency she said that meant no offence to India and hoped that he would stick to his decision to visit India. On the occasion of the American bicentennial she sent a thousand word message of good will to the *Time* magazine saying that India truly valued friendship with the USA.[26]

A bicentennial volume giving history of interactions between the two countries during the last 200 years was prepared by an eminent journalist M.V. Kamath at the instance of the Indian embassy in Washington. The volume written in an extremely lucid style, was opulently produced and profusely illustrated. It was nostalgically recalled how Columbus in his mission to discover India discovered America never realising that a day would come when these two nations would play pivotal role in harmonising the cultural heritage of the East and the West. At a function held on 22 July 1976, the volume was presented to the Speaker of the House of Representatives, Carl Albert.

As a reciprocatory gesture, President Ford, through the retiring ambassador T.N. Kaul, sent for Mrs. Gandhi a specially carved American redwood plaque on the occasion of the bicentennial year. The plaque bore the symbol of America, bald head eagle, and carried the legend, 'out of many one' as a symbol of friendship and cooperation between the peoples of the two countries.

Jimmy Carter's election was welcomed in India so that he may start his tenure with a sense of goodwill. His administration in its message to Congress on human rights was not unsympathetic towards India when it referred to the situation in that country. It conceded the known facts of authoritarian rule which in case of India was treated with a gloss. There was nothing strange in this sort of US stand. Despite its proclaimed views on human rights President Carter was visiting and doing business with Iran and Saudi Arabia; so was he carrying on nicely with Brazil and some other Latin American countries and South Africa which, in no way, could claim to be upholders of human rights. As a statesman he had to realize that in asserting the value of observance of human rights he could not go beyond a certain style as, otherwise, it would recoil adversely on the US national interest.

## REFERENCES

1. K. Ramaswamy in *Assam Tribune*, 6 December 1972.
2. *Hindustan Times*, 10 February 1972 also 13 August 1972.
3. *International Herald Tribune*, 6 July 1972. (cited in P. Sahadevan p. 653).
4. *Times of India*, 16 March 1973.
5. P. Sahdevan, *Indo-US Relations* (in M.S. Rajan's second volume, p. 506).
6. *Asian Recorder*, 9-15 April 1975 p. 12534-5.
7. Ibid.
8. *Hindu*, 16 July 1973 from Easwar Sagar in Washington.

9. *Hindu*, 23 June 1974.

10. *Tribune*, 21 September 1974.

11. The affirmation was made by President Nixon when Pakistan Minister of Defence Aziz Ahmed raised the issue of Indian blast. See *Hindustan Times*, 25 May 1974.

12. Statement made by Senator Charles Percy on his visit to India see *Motherland*, 6 September 1974.

13. Washington *Star News*, 8 September 1974.

14. Remark of Pell on 21 January 1975. Congressional Record 1975 p. 30207. Both cited in A.P. Rana (ed.) *Four Decades of Indo-US Relations*, p. 189.

15. *Mainstream*, 2 November 1974, p. 5, editorial 'Kissinger's conviction'.

16. *Hindustan Times*, 31 October 1974.

17. *Hindu*, 31 October 1974 from G.K. Reddy.

18. Ibid.

19. *Mainstream*, 2 November 1974, op. cit.

20. For the text of the agreement and the joint communique issued at the end of Kissinger's visit see *Foreign Affairs Record* vol. 20 (1974) pp. 284-286.

21. *Times of India*, 18 September 1975.

22. Warren Unna in the *Statesman*, 26 September 1975.

23. *Hindustan Times*, 19 September 1975.

24. *Hindu*, 5 August 1976.

25. *Hindustan Times*, 25 October 1976.

26. Ibid. 28 October 1976.

# 4

# Janata Regime

The year 1977 marked the stage when the relations between the two countries were expected to be cordial. It is in the beginning of the year that the new President, a nominee of the Democratic party, Jimmy Carter assumed office replacing Gerald Ford of the Republican party. Consequently Henry Kissinger lost his position as Secretary of State to Cyrus Vance. Correspondingly, in March 1977 elections in India, the Congress party was defeated by the Janata party causing a change in the complexion of the government headed by Morarji Desai. During the election campaign, Janata leaders reiterated their resolve to follow the policy of genuine non alignment correcting the tilt which was said to be in favour of the Soviet Union.[1]

The advent of Janata regime was widely welcomed by the American people and media. President Carter praised India for practising democracy in choice of its leadership. In this context it may be recalled that during preceding regimes the Bangladesh crisis remained a big hurdle. The peaceful explosion of an atomic device created further misunderstanding and finally, the imposition of the emergency made the matters worse. With these events now going into the limbo of history, a new era opened which seemed to augur better relations between the two countries. President Carter in greeting Morarji Desai hoped to see the end of the troubled phase of the Indo-US relations.[2]

The statement of goodwill was followed by some concrete steps to give practical form to what were mere sentiments. First the US Senate Foreign Relations Committee voted on 31 March 1977 to repeal an anti-India amendment requiring the US representatives to the World Bank to vote against low interest loans to India. Secondly, at the instance of the State Department, the US Nuclear Regulatory Commission (NRC) approved in July 1977 the sale and shipment to India of 12.261 kg. of enriched uranium to meet the refuelling needs of Tarapur power plant for six months.[3] Thirdly, the US took a favourable position at the Aid India Consortium meeting held in Paris in 1977 to decide India's share of the International Development Association's Funds. Finally, in July 1977 the US budget included an allocation of $ 60 million for assistance to India. The provisions of this aid were in recognition of the significance of re-establishment of democratic principles and restoration of political freedom in India after the defeat of Mrs. Gandhi. In the new political environment the Consortium felt well disposed to increase the aid from $ 1670 million to $ 2300 million in 1977.[4]

A negative factor which helped India was President Carter's decision to end Washington's earlier tilt towards Pakistan. What annoyed Carter personally was Bhutto's public denunciation that he was ousted from power by a conspiracy which was hatched with Carter's approval.[5] India felt benefited a little by the US adopting a realistic attitude towards the two countries of South Asia. India, on its part, tried to reciprocate the gesture of good will initiated by Carter administration. Morarji took the first opportunity to assure his American counterpart that India was determined to pursue the nuclear policy exclusively for peaceful purposes and that his government would conduct no more nuclear tests[6].

This happy mood was further witnessed in the official visit of Warren Christopher, Deputy Secretary of State on 23 July 1977. During his talks with the Indian leaders he tried to highlight the issues on which the two countries could work amicably with due regard to the mutual interests of the two countries. His country acknowledged India's pre-eminence in South Asia and hoped it would take up the position of leadership in the region. He assured that the US would resume its bilateral economic aid and would step up the trade between the two countries. Finally, he stressed that the US nuclear policy was designed for world wide application and not for compelling any particular country to fall in line with its concept of non-proliferation. Vajpayee gave a very cordial speech in his honour in which he expected that the US administration would give up some old tilts and prejudices. He welcomed the hand of friendship that was extended by the new American President and assured of India's commitment to the basic approach of independence of judgement and detachment from blocs. Now with the strength of popular support with which they came to power, they would be free from bias and be friendly to all who valued our friendship.[7]

**Carter's Visit**

The US President Jimmy Carter arrived here in the early afternoon on 1 January 1978 after a brief halt at Teheran. On arrival he declared that he was delighted to begin the new year in India and make new friends in a country that shared his deep faith in basic moral values and firm dedication to world peace. His feeling of admiration for India he had inherited from his mother who had worked with great dedication as a nurse in a village in Gurgaon (Haryana) where she was posted as a peace corps volunteer.

Speaking of the 'unbreakable bonds of friendship' between India and the USA Morarji Desai, welcomed President Carter not only as the head of a friendly nation that shared the same values but also as a symbol of dedication to high human ideals that brought the two countries together despite the vast distance that separated them. The very fact that President Carter had chosen to spend the new year's day in India indicated that he considered this country a sort of home away from home. President Carter spoke of Morarji in glowing terms as a man of great courage, rectitude and dedication. What was significant about his statement was his work to see that the people of other countries get benefited from 'our consultation, our standards of moral values and our hopes of world peace'.

The platitudinous references to common ideals and aspirations on the occasion of a state visit are an essential preamble to more intensive discussions on issues that united or separated the two peoples. Carter plainly said that he had come primarily to dispel accumulated legacies of misunderstanding, irritants and cross purposes of the past. Carter gave the impression that he was a different kind of President who had come to get a whiff of the new ethos of India that was seeking to solve its problem in its own way and find its rightful place in a rapidly changing world.[8] However, the real significance of Indo-US dialogue lay in the fact that after a long period of agonising self-reappraisal and self-criticism the US had started rediscovering itself and regaining its lost confidence.

Morarji Desai was stoic as usual in standing firm on what he considered India's enlightened self interest without being much affected by the exaggerated reaffirmation of common ideas and higher values of life to which the two countries professed to be committed. He utilised the first opportunity to reiterate India's nuclear policy in his own characteristic style by referring to the twin evils of atomic bomb and atmospheric pollution which President Carter was committed to banish in course of time.[9]

Apart from the nuclear question, which was the main point of contention the issues that figured at the Indo-American summit included the future of Sino-Indian relations, West Asian problems, the Indian Ocean affairs, the evils of racism in South Africa and the prospects of increased Indo-US bilateral cooperation. Even on the nuclear issue while Desai reiterated his country's opposition to a blanket acceptance of safeguards he agreed with Carter on the need for nuclear disarmament. Carter told Desai that Britain and Soviet Union were moving towards a comprehensive nuclear test ban treaty, including peaceful experiments. It was his hope that France and China too would finally be persuaded to accept it. Desai warmly reacted to it and said that if the USA and USSR reached an agreement it would positively influence and promote the process of disarmament.[10]

In his address to the members of Parliament, Carter assured that the US administration had authorised the shipment of 7.5 tons of enriched uranium to tide over the crisis created by the accident in the heavy water plant at Baroda. As regards the status of the contractual obligation. President Carter's press secretary Jody Powell was evasive but he assured that the new legislation would not cover the past constraints. The new legislation would be implemented in a phased manner with restrictions on the administrative power becoming operative in 24 months from the date of its being passed by the Congress.[11]

As regards China, the two sides agreed that efforts be made to improve relations with that country without prejudice to their established friendship with other nations. This was the point that President Reddy had earlier made in his banquet speech. The Indian side heard with interest the reassuring impression that Carter gave of steady progress in the US talks with the Soviet Union over the limitation of arms race in the Indian Ocean. Carter's press secretary J. Powell said it was the historic expression of concern on the part of India in avoiding military confrontation in the Indian Ocean that had first brought the issue to the notice of President Carter.

During the course of conversation, Carter asked Desai why India had not exchanged ambassadors with Israel while its policy was one of amity with all countries. Desai replied that full diplomatic relations would follow peace in West Asia. India had allowed Israel to have a consulate in Bombay so that non-political relations could be carried out. He firmly told Carter that there would be no early peace in West Asia until

Israel vacated occupied Arab territory and met the just demand of Palestinians to have their own independent state.[12]

Since the nuclear issue became dominant in the bilateral relationship, the political climate between the two countries did not favour a discussion of significant areas of economic cooperation. Before the Carter visit expectation was that the nuclear controversy would be set aside and some tangible areas of cooperation highlighted. But what happened was the unexpected. India had asked its ambassador in Washington to probe the prospect of securing the US support to the Ganga-Cauvery project involving an outlay of about Rs. 150000 million.[13] This project was going to be India's ambitious rural thrust in the Gangetic plain and for the strategic north-south region. This along with other projects was marginalised.

Now it appeared that the nuclear controversy had to be settled in one way or the other before meaningful cooperation in other areas was pursued. Detailed talks on this issue were held during Carter's visit. Carter's main object was to secure 'safeguards' from India, that is India's consent to international inspection of its nuclear plants. But Desai was very firm in stating that the nuclear super powers had morally no right to seek to impose full scope safeguards on recipients of nuclear materials while they themselves refused to accept those conditions. What was paradoxical was that while they had been daily adding to their stockpile of nuclear weapons, they were advising non-nuclear powers like India to accept full scope safeguards even for development of nuclear energy for peaceful purposes.[14]

It was too much to expect of the two super powers to come to an agreement to destroy their stock piles of nuclear weapons and accept full scope safeguards themselves. This was discussed in detail by the two leaders and they tried to evolve some solution to this potential conflict about international safeguards on production of nuclear power versus adequate supply of fuel. According to Carter, one possibility that they could explore was that if the two super powers could conclude a comprehensive test ban treaty, it would be an adequate factor for India to accept comprehensive safeguards without having to violate the principles of autonomy or independence.[15]

Carter was surprised by the firm stand that Desai took on this issue. This was confirmed by a transcript of Carter's conversation with Secretary of State Cyrus Vana in which he said 'Mr. Desai was pretty adamant about the nuclear fuel — when we get back, I think we ought to write him another letter, just cold and very blunt.' Later in a press interview Carter admitted that he regretted that the mike incident was a 'gaffe' but an inadvertent one. He admitted that it should not have occurred but it caused no problem between him and Desai. In a way it helped both of them. Carter wanted Indians to know what the Congress was going to do within next 18 months. He was referring to the Nuclear Proliferation Act which was before the Congress and which stipulated severe action against those countries that did not accept full scope safeguards. Carter wanted Desai to know that the Congress was going to pass 'strengthened requirements' on fuel supply and this would affect India also. Carter later talked about what the US was willing to do in the way of supplying nuclear fuel. 'I told him I would authorise transfer of fuel, but it did not seem to make an impression on him' Carter said in a very rough passage on the tape.[16]

The joint declaration signed by the two leaders reaffirmed the unwavering faith of the two countries in the democratic form of government and respect for basic human rights while pledging them to work together to end the economic disparities and enrich the quality of life through a better utilisation of the planet's resources. The 500 word declaration confined to the enunciation of the lofty principles that were universal in their appeal. This was quite different both in the style and content from similar documents signed by India with other countries. The declaration made no reference at all to any bilateral issues other than their proclaimed faith in democratic values and human rights.[17]

Carter's aim was to convince his Indian hosts that there was a new administration in the USA whose approach to foreign policy affairs was different from the previous ones. With regard to India, his visit was to set a public seal on the end of notorious Nixon's tilt against India. Now Washington would no longer look upon the subcontinent as an area in which Indian position had to be counter balanced by some other country. During talks Carter made explicit references recognising the pre-eminent position which India had come to occupy in the sub continent. This view was endorsed by Brezezinsky, President's security adviser who said that it was impossible not to mention India as a regional power in South Asia exercising influence on some key countries and also balancing others.[18]

Analysing the aspirations of the two countries in upholding some moral values of political life Carter said in Parliament that not long ago both of their governments passed through grave crisis which threatened the basic values for the protection of which many a people gave their lives. He was obviously referring to the excesses committed during the emergency period in India and the Watergate scandal in the USA which shook the conscience of the people in both the countries. Both faced them by different means and on opposite sides of the world to witness in the end the triumph of moral values to which the people of both the countries stood committed.[19]

The immediate impression that Carter's visit gave was that the two leaders established a personal rapport. Desai found in Carter a warm and well meaning statesman who meant well to those who sought his sympathy and good will for some deserving causes. Though at times they tended to give the impression of talking like two Popes as to who was nearer to God, the dominant impression they had created was of an intensive desire and commitment to serve their respective people and through them the rest of mankind in their own way.[20]

President Carter was realist enough to realise his limitations. He did not assume the airs of a reformer or a crusader. It was quite evident from the matter of fact way he went through various engagements that he had not come to resolve every difference of approach and opinion all at once but only to hold out an ennobling vision of a happier world free from avoidable tension and undue exploitation. As for the future relations between the two countries, it was not as if they were going to see eye to eye on all issues or that even if there was agreement results would be automatic and genuine. On the contrary, differences would persist, for instance, on nuclear policy. But such differences would not vitiate or stop the forward movement in other directions. What was notable about Carter's visit was that the unmistakable atmosphere of goodwill it had generated all round might well be the beginning of a new chapter in Indo-American relations.

**Morarji Desai's Visit**

Morarji Deseai reached New York on 8 June to address the UN General Assembly on disarmament and later to pay the return visit of President Carter. Before reaching Washington Desai paid a two-day visit to San Francisco to meet Indian community there. It is there that in pre-independence days, the Ghadar party was founded to carry on the message of Indian struggle of independence. From there he flew back to New York, where another gathering of Indian community heard him speak on how they should look at India of their times. At these meetings he tried to educate both Indians and Americans on issues he was going to discuss with Carter administration.

He reached Washington on 12 June where he remained busy for two days in discussions with President Carter, his top officials and the Congressmen. In his welcome remarks Carter referred to the restoration of democracy in India and Desai's role in it, as one of the significant events of the decade. It was a remarkable coincidence that the end of the trauma of the 19-month old emergency in India should have occurred about the same time that the Carter administration with its equally firm commitment to democracy, clean politics and respect for the dignity of the individual had made its advent in the US.[21]

The talks were wide range covering on all international issues in which the two countries were interested. To start with, Desai tried to set at rest all the doubts that were in the mind of President Carter by assuring him that India's interest was in seeing that Pakistan remained strong and stable since a weak Pakistan would become a problem for India. He narrated the steps India had taken to improve its relations with Pakistan though the latter was not responsive.

About China he said that if that country took one step forward, we would take two on the path of normalisation of relations between the two countries. India was an aggrieved party and it was for China to be realist in approaching the border dispute. Though China's anti-India activities in the border lands had abated, it had made no move to reconcile the old differences which were quite serious. Another issue that came up during discussion was America's hope that India would not go ahead with its intention to buy some $ 2 billion worth of sophisticated deep penetrating fighter aircrafts from the Soviet Union lest this would escalate the arms race in the subcontinent particularly in regard to Pakistan.[22] Desai was adamant on this suggestion. 'We are not in arms race at all. We are only replacing planes which will become obsolete in three to four years. We are replacing seven squadrons with five squadrons thus reducing and not increasing the strength of the airforce'; Desai firmly said.[23]

About Soviet and Cuban forces in Africa, Desai said that all outside forces should get out of Africa even though the Cubans were 'invited' by Ethiopia. India would not accept such an invitation and did not think it a very good idea for others to do so. It was a hard line against the Soviet and Cuban forces that Carter himself had been taking but Desai's views strengthened his stand.

When Desai was asked why India had not exchanged diplomats with Israel, he said he did not know the reason for the then Prime Minister's thinking and implied that he was neither responsible nor necessarily in agreement with what had been done by the previous government. At that stage it would not be useful to suddenly start changing India's West Asian relations by entertaining a diplomatic exchange with Israel while that country's relations with the Arabs were so unsettled. Before India could take any step in this direction, Israel must come to terms with its Arab neighbours.[24]

On nuclear issue, Desai categorically assured that India would not produce nuclear weapons nor would it continue nuclear tests even for peaceful purposes. This would reassure India's neighbours, particularly Pakistan which called the 1974 explosion as a 'nuclear blackmail'. Desai gave the assurance that his successors would follow the same nuclear policy. If they did not, the US could reconsider its position as a fuel supplier. About India's nuclear assistance programme Desai made it clear that India only assisted friendly countries in purely peaceful methods with technology appropriate to each country concerned. India would not give any thing that might be conducive to military use. India would be more than willing to sign a comprehensive test ban treaty if the USA and the Soviet Union agreed on such a treaty provided it was not discriminatory.

The main point of disagreement in Indo-American relations was the nuclear issue. President Carter told Desai that the main obstacle to gaining approval for further enriched uranium shipments for Tarapur during the next 18 months grace period of the Nuclear Non-proliferation Act lay with the Congress and that it was Congress which had the lead over the US President in foreign policy matters. Yet it was President Carter who originally urged Congress to enact the law which deprived recipients of US nuclear material and technology if they failed to open up all their nuclear facilities, including those that were not US-assisted, to international inspection.

Both sides were engaged in finding some solution to international inspection which India considered discriminatory because it did not apply to the nations which already had nuclear weapons. Desai said that before India agreed to international inspection the nuclear 'haves' specifically the USA and the Soviet Union, must first stop testing, stop increasing their nuclear arsenals and start cutting back towards ultimate scrapping of the nuclear weapons they already had.

However, the controversy was nearly solved when the House of Representatives Committee on International Relations permitted the shipment of Tarapur fuel on 14 June and the Senate followed suit on 20 June. But both Houses simultaneously warned that the future supplies would be cut off if India did not agree to full scope safeguards within 18 months. The talks that Desai had with members of both the Houses, facilitated the approval of the Tarapur shipment which might have been further delayed.[25] The present shipment gave the Indian scientists time up to 1980 to perfect the technology of refining nuclear fuel. Thereafter India may not need any American help in this connection.

The Congress agreed to sanction the sales so that the deal would continue to maintain US leverage on negotiations with India on new safeguards against nuclear proliferation. But Desai's views were different, he told the Congressmen that India would not sign the nuclear proliferation treaty just to get 7.6 tons of uranium. He reminded that the contract signed by the US fifteen years ago was still binding and it should not be arbitrarily subjected to any outside considerations.

The nuclear non-proliferation act of 1978 violated the agreement and if agreements are violated in such a manner, there would be no sanctity of any other agreement which may be signed subsequently. He made it quite clear that till the time the USA broke its agreement or there was a breach in its constitutional obligation, India would not look for alternative source of nuclear fuel. But once a breach was caused India would have no difficulty in finding out alternative ways. He finally added that if once the plutonium producing plants were open to international inspection, and all military reactors were converted into civilian reactors there was no problem about India's accepting full scope safeguards and even signing the NPT.

Bearing these points in view the Congress endorsed the recommendations of their sub committees permitting an 18 month period until 1980 that the differences may be resolved over the controversial clauses of international inspection. A remarkable fact about this discussion was that some of the Congressmen who had been steadfastly opposed to the supply of Tarapur fuel were the very ones that not only voted but actively campaigned for a favourable decision on the export licence in the House's International Committee. This agreeable result came not through any special concessions that Desai had to make but through renewed faith in India's credibility as projected by him. Unfortunately the US Congress had always sensed a gap between India's professions and practices; the suspicion had always existed that India's definition of morality was more rigorous for others. This impression had now been corrected at least, with regard to the government headed by Desai.[26]

A joint communique issued on 15 June at the end of Desai's visit reported wide areas of agreement between the two countries on issues discussed during their talks. The two leaders discussed measures to ensure non-proliferation of nuclear weapons including appropriate means of ensuring that nuclear energy was not misused for military purpose. Regarding bilateral relations, President Carter pledged to make every effort consistent with American laws to maintain the fuel supplies for Tarapur plant and continue nuclear cooperation with India. Although the pending US shipment of 7.6 tons of nuclear fuel was cleared further supplies of enriched uranium were considered unlikely because the new US laws restricted export of nuclear fuel to countries which did not accept full scope safeguards.[27] One significant point added in the communique was with regard to the measures to be adopted to expand economic cooperation between the two countries. Mrs. Juanila Kreps, the US Commerce Secretary would visit India later in the year to explore the substantial potential for expanding the economic exchanges between the two countries. The International Executive Service Corps would appoint a highly qualified retired American businessman to pursue the Indo-US Business Council's plans for promoting cooperation between India and US commercial organisations in the construction of engineering projects in other countries.

## REFERENCES

1. *Indian Express*, 23 March 1977
2. *Washington Post*, 23 March 1977
3. P. Sahdevan op. cit., p. 520.
4. *Patriot*, 18 June 1977
5. *International Herald Tribune*, 13-14 August 1977
6. P. Sahdevan op. cit., p. 522.
7. Ibid
8. *Hindu*, 2 January 1978 from G.K. Reddy.
9. Ibid
10. *Stateman*, 3 January 1978
11. *Hindustan Times*, 3 January 1978
12. Kuldip Nayar in *Times* (London), 5 January 1978
13. Ashok Kapur in *Nagpur Times*, 18 January 1978 a Syndicated article
14. *Amrit Bazar Patrika*, 19 January 1978, edit: 'Desai reiterates stand'
15. *Times of India*, 14 January 1978 from M.V. Kamath in Washington

16. Ajit Bhattacharjea, 'President Carter's indiscretion', *Indian Express*, 7 January 1978
17. *Hindu*, 4 January 1978 from G.K. Reddy
18. Pran Chopra in the '*Pioneer*', 8 January 1978
19. See *Statesman*, 4 January 1978, edit: 'Carter Once again'
20. *Hindu*, 3 January 1978, from G.K. Reddy
21. *Hindu*, 14 June 1978
22. *Statesman*, 15 June 1978 from Warrem Unna
23. Ibid
24. Ibid. 19 June 1978
25. Hirnamay Karlekar 'the US visit and after' *Hindustan Times*, 30 June 1978
26. N.C. Menon in *Hindustan Times*, 23 June 1978
27. *Indian Express*, 16 June 1978 from T.V. Parasuram

# 5

# The Afghan Crisis

The entry of 40,000 Soviet troops in Afghanistan on 27 December 1979 at the alleged invitation by the Soviet supported regime of Babrak Karnal was viewed by President Carter with great concern. He linked the Soviet armed intervention in Afghanistan with the general crisis in the Persian Gulf region for which he held Moscow responsible. The collapse of the monarchy in Iran in February 1979 and its take over by a bitterly anti-US Islamic fanatic, Ayatollah Khomenie was an ominous development which subsequently led to the storming of the American embassy in Teheran by his young cohorts and taking 50 US employees as hostages in protest against the asylum given to the former king of Iran. All this was still fresh in American mind. Now the US administration started realising that the US forces could not stop a Soviet threat towards the Gulf through Iran unless some steps to fortify the area were taken.

As an immediate reaction President Carter at a press conference on 28 December 1979 described the Soviet military intervention in Afghanistan as a grave threat to peace. The same day the National Security Council observed that the Soviet occupation of Afghanistan created a threat to both Iran and Pakistan and would soon drastically modify the balance of power in favour of the Soviet Union. In their view it was an extension of Brezhnev doctrine and qualitatively a new event in that it was the first time since World War II that the Soviet Union had used its own armed forces beyond the Warsaw pact sphere to impose its authority over a third world country.[1]

In the President's annual State of the Union address on 23 January 1980, President Carter enunciated what came to be known later as Carter doctrine. He referred in his message, to an attempt made by an outside power to gain control of the Persian Gulf region's oil supply which was an assault on the vital interests of the USA. In the larger context, Carter viewed it as a serious threat to peace since the second world war to stem which he suggested some punitive measures be taken such as the blocking the export of 17 million tons of grains, stopping the sale of high technology equipments, delaying the opening of the new Soviet consulate in New York, postponing talks of cultural programme and boycotting the Moscow Olympics, the last action later joined by Germany, Japan and China.[2]

The policy adopted by Carter was also pursued by Reagan in garnering all national resources whose collective pressure would force the Soviet Union to withdraw from Afghanistan. The process, in his view, would be hastened if the resistance by the rebels would get strengthened for which the US was prepared to contribute its share. As regards the nature of aid actually extended by the USA to the Mujahideens, it was mostly financial which by the end of 1985 had gone up to $ 650 million. By a Congressional legislation passed in that year, the administration paid $ 470 million in 1986 and $ 630 million in 1987. Besides, the US Agency for International Development provided $ 40 million by 1988 for helping the refugees displaced by the fighting.[3] In all during the 1980s the US funelled well more than $ 2 billion in money and weapons to the rebels. It was the largest covert action programme since the second world war. Supply levels rose from 10,000 tons in 1983 to 65000 tons in 1987.[4] Another important help was rendered by the CIA officials who collaborated with Pak intelligence service personnel. The CIA had also started a covert operation to supply weapons to

Afghan rebels. It was the largest CIA operation to supply weapons to Afghan rebels. The rebels were also supplied arms obtained from Egypt, China and Iran through Pakistan. What was, after all, the American strategy in the Afghan crisis? The leadership was guided by a Pentagon report which warned the American leadership to keep in mind that in the midst of anti-American wave in Iran, the Soviet Union would exploit the political turmoil in Iran to change the world balance of power. Moscow would also like to control Persian Gulf to give a mortal blow to the American interests in the region. It was a warning to be aware of the region being the most likely flash point for confrontation between the US and Soviet Union.

The US was not prepared to go to the length of coming to a direct war with the Soviet Union. They wanted to achieve their objective by a more subtle move that is by supplying the latest weapons to the anti-Kabul forces to escalate the conflict. In that case, the Soviet Union would be forced to commit more and more forces in the country. Once the Soviet Union was caught in the quagmire of Afghanistan conflict, it would be bled white. There were visions of Afghanistan turning into a Vietnam in which, it was recalled, the US remained embroiled for over two decades. Similar debacle Moscow was going to face in Afghanistan it was the general impression in political circles in those countries which were vitally affected by this crisis.

The US also presumed that prolonged fighting in Afghanistan would discredit the Soviet Union in the third world countries. With Russia involved in the Afghan crisis, its pressure on West Asia and East Europe would be much reduced. Taking advantage of the Soviet threat, the US would be able to resume arms supplies to Pakistan and secure bases in that country. The US also hoped to persuade the Persian Gulf countries to extend more facilities to the US armed forces. The littoral states may allow the US to strengthen its bases on the Diego Garcia and coral islands in the Indian Ocean. These were some of the plus points in the US calculation with which it would face the Soviet challenge in Afghanistan.

President Carter also tried to mobilise allies and friends in support of his confrontation policy towards Soviet intervention in Afghanistan. But he met with little success as most of them had trade relations with the Soviet Union which would be adversely affected by their adopting an anti-Soviet policy and that too for a cause for which they had no genuine sympathy. At a meeting in Brussels in January 1980, EEC foreign ministers failed to agree on a common line to be taken with regard to the Soviet Union. The only consensus to emerge was a statement condemning the Soviet intervention in Afghanistan and calling for immediate withdrawal of Soviet troops. Carter's disappointment found expression in his warning to the allies in Rome in June that Europe could not be an island of detente implying that tension may also grip the continent. The West European countries felt that their alliance would be severely strained if they faithfully echoed the voice of America.[5]

## II

When the Soviet intervention in Afghanistan took place India was being governed by the care-taker government headed by Charan Singh. The country was in the midst of election campaign which had taken away the External Affairs Minister S.N. Mishra to some distant place in his native state, Bihar. So the matter was left to be dealt with by the officials of the External Affairs Ministry.

On his own initiative the Soviet ambassador Yuri Yoronstov called on Ram Sathe Foreign Secretary on 28 December and handed over to him a message from the Soviet government informing him that at the request of the Afghan leadership, Moscow had sent to Afghanistan a small military force to enable Kabul to resist external aggression and interference. He further assured that the dispatch of the Soviet forces was in terms of the Soviet-Afghan treaty as well as Article 51 of the UN Charter which provided for individual or collective self defence in the case of an external armed attack.[6] He had the guts to tell our Foreign Secretary that the Soviet action could be likened to India's armed intervention in Bangladesh in 1971.

However, a few hours later, the government issued a note in which it was clearly stated that as a country committed to the principle of non alignment, India supported the sovereign right of the Afghan people to determine their own destiny free from foreign interference, the Government of India was opposed to any outside interference in the internal affairs of one country by another; the government also hoped that no external power would take steps which might aggravate the situation and that normalization would be restored in Afghanistan as early as possible.[7] As regards India's reaction to the entry of the Soviet troops the official spokesman said that the government was observing the situation and assessing whether the Soviet assumption that they extended their help on the request of the duly constituted authorities in Kabul was right or wrong. The government even admitted that they were ignorant as to who invited the Soviet intervention.[8]

India was worried by this development in a neighbouring country with which it had close relations but what caused more concern was the fact that Pakistan was being rapidly and very heavily rearmed by the US. On 30 December, Prime Minister Charan Singh received a letter from President Carter drawing India's attention to the seriousness of the Soviet action but making no reference to his decision to lift the embargo on the transfer of arms to Pakistan.[9] The same day the US ambassador was called in the Ministry and told that the supply of arms to Pakistan would increase tension in South Asia and hurt the process that was going on for the normalisation of relations between India and Pakistan that were shattered in the war of December 1971; it would also delay the restoration of normalization in Afghanistan.

On the same day the Prime Minister sent for the Soviet ambassador and told him that the presence of Soviet troops in Afghanistan would have far reaching adverse consequences for the South Asian region and expressed the hope that

Moscow would recall its troops as soon as possible. On 2 January Charan Singh in his reply to Carter, expressed India's 'total opposition', to the American decision to transfer arms to Pakistan. He was a little strident in telling him that the US may not 'relapse in to the old misguided policy' of arming Pakistan in response to a temporary phase of a crisis in Afghanistan. The supply of arms to Pakistan would have the least relevance to the larger interests of the subcontinent at a time when after decades of suspicion and animosity interspersed with two armed conflicts between India and Pakistan bilateral relations had been improving steadily. In his view, the US decision would undermine a potential non aligned initiative which may induce Pakistan to deal with the Afghanistan developments more realistically.[10]

Another development in this context should also be noted. When the issue was referred to the Security Council, the Soviet Union vetoed an American move to censure the intervention. Some US allies took the issue to the General Assembly of the UN where a 17-nation resolution was moved, among others, by Pakistan and Bangladesh for immediate withdrawal of all foreign troops from Afghanistan. The Indian envoy made a statement on 11 January 1980 in which he said that India had received assurances from Moscow that the intervention had been at the specific request of Afghanistan government and that the Soviet troops could be withdrawn when the Kabul regime asked for it. India, he added, had no reason to disbelieve a friendly country. But he stressed that India was concerned about the attempts of outside powers to interfere in the internal affairs of Afghanistan by training, arming and encouraging subversive elements to create disturbances in that country. India was interested in the peace of the region which would be possible only if independence and non alignment of Afghanistan remained undisturbed.

In the first week of Mrs. Gandhi's return to power, the US ambassador was called in and told that the US decision to arm Pakistan in the wake of Soviet intervention in Afghanistan would not improve matters but would escalate tension in the subcontinent. The ambassador tried to reassure that the proposed arms transfer to Pakistan was designed to improve the 'general security environment' in the region rather than to strengthen the military muscles of Pakistan. He was naive to believe that the Indian sentiments would be pacified if he offered to dangle a few carrots. Accordingly, the envoy expressed US readiness to meet India's defence requirements in specific spheres without imposing any pre-conditions. He also offered to discuss how to ensure early dispatch of two friendly shipments of American nuclear fuel for the Tarapur plant.[11] American assumption that by these incentives India would acquiesce to the arming of Pakistan was misplaced.

Indian point of view was that Carter's diplomatic operations ignored New Delhi's sensitivities from beginning to end. He sent his national security assistant Brezeinski and deputy secretary of state, Warren Chistopher to Pakistan but picked up only a special envoy in the person of Clark Clifford to go to New Delhi. The simultaneous dispatch of two unequal missions revealed to Indians the relative importance that Carter gave to the role of India and Pakistan in the Soviet intervention in Afghanistan. As was expected Clifford's talks with Mrs. Gandhi and the External Affairs Minister Narsimha Rao turned out to be quite barren as both sides had different perceptions of the Afghan crisis. Clifford's focus was on the Soviet intervention which compelled the US to offer military aid to Pakistan. Indian leaders stressed on the danger the US arms aid to Pakistan would pose to the subcontinent. Clifford, later at a press conference reaffirmed that any further move by the Soviet Union to reach out to the Persian Gulf would mean war.[12] He also warned that if the Soviets felt tempted to go to Pakistan, then that would also bring grave difficulties. But he assured that the Americans would be there to ascertain that the arms were used in the way they were intended. Clifford left New Delhi with the impression that it was difficult for India and the US to reconcile their views on Afghan crisis.

Indian leadership was dismayed by the performance of Clifford during his visit to India but it was shocking to hear Kissinger saying on 22 January 1980 that it was extremely unlikely that the Soviets would attack Pakistan and warned that the real threat would develop if the Soviet Union and India cooperated. 'We must of course do our best to prevent this from happening. But the greatest danger was that India may seek, with Soviet cooperation, to dismember its neighbour by splitting Baluchistan and North West Frontier Province and by occupying (Pakistan occupied) Kashmir. Both India and the Soviet Union would then be surrounded by weak client states; a serious policy must deal with that contingency; Kissinger warned with the suggestion that the US air borne units be stationed in Pakistan for an interim period to meet an emergency.

The long term US plan was that apart from re-equipping some of the existing Pakistani formations to improve their mobility, fire power and communication system, be raised over the next two years to double the deployment along the Afghan border without reducing its present strength on the Indian front. The US strategy was to build up Pakistan's military strength on the Afghan border to a point where Pakistan could absorb the first shock of a Soviet attack until the US air and naval forces stepped in to stem the advance. The US policy was not to get directly involved in the war otherwise it would be another Korean war, this time in a different region to assist Pakistan and Afghanistan rebels to fight it out for themselves.

Mrs. Gandhi's government opened channels of diplomatic dialogue with countries within and outside the region with a view to explaining them the possibility of an initiative that would induce the Soviets to pull out the bulk of their troops from Afghanistan within a relatively short time. The diplomatic soundings did not hold out much hope of any joint initiative for exerting collective pressure on the super powers to desist from further involvement in the affairs of the region. India did not expect a common regional stand on the

Afghan crisis to emerge from its diplomatic endeavours but it was keen on creating a better awareness among the neighbouring countries of the inherent danger of a much bigger crisis before long if nothing was done to discourage the developing confrontation between the super powers. India was also reported to have thought of convening a conference of the foreign ministers of a few countries concerned with this crisis to discuss what could be done to avert the danger of big power rivalries in the region. But, again for want of favourable response from those who were supposed to exercise their influence on the powers involved in the crisis, the Indian initiative remained a mere idea.

However, India's diplomatic forays had their desired impact on world public opinion. Between January and April 1980, more than 30 foreign dignitaries came to New Delhi mainly to discuss the Afghan developments with Indian leaders. They came from all continents, representing great, medium and small powers, governments of all political colours, belonging to all existing alignments and groupings. The prominent among them were the UN Secretary General, the President of France and Austria, the Foreign Ministers of USSR, Britain, Italy and Romania, the Prime Minister of Vietnam and Foreign Minister of Cuba and Algeria and the leaders of PLO. Mrs. Gandhi and her Foreign Minister Narasimha Rao spent over 130 hours in discussing the various issues related to the Afghan crisis with the foreign guests. But the US did not send a senior officer of the State Department to New Delhi. Rao did talk to the Secretary of State Cyprus Vance in Washington. Mrs. Gandhi met Zia ul-Haq, Hua Guofeng and Leonid Brezhnev in Salesbury and Belgrade.[13]

The US viewed these developments quite seriously as it considered itself to be the target of Indian criticism. As a result of persistent probing, India could succeed in blockading the US-Pakistan arms deal. When Gonslave was in Washington the deal had not fallen though it had run into some difficulties. India wanted to move a little closer to the

US position about the basis of normalising the Afghan situation but was aware that the Soviets would neither make a token withdrawal nor announce a time table for military pullout without adequate reciprocal gesture from the US.[14]

In the last week of February 1980, Mrs. Gandhi sent Eric Gonsalve, Secretary in the Ministry of External Affairs to Washington to meet several senior officers in the State Department. In his long discussions with them he gave a gist of Mrs. Gandhi's conversation with Gromyko and tried to seek a meeting of Soviet and American perceptions of the Afghan situation. He was happy to observe that there was a change in the American attitude towards the crisis, the US was now seeking a diplomatic rather than a military settlement. He was assured by US officials that the administration had not taken any major decision about arms transfer to Pakistan. On his return Gonsalve conveyed his impressions to Mrs. Gandhi that the Afghan crisis had reached its climax; now it would de-escalate. Both the super powers had realised the futility of confrontation on an issue which could be settled by direct dialogues; now they were inclined towards that goal.

The diplomatic stalemate could not last for ever. In early March it came to the notice of Indian foreign office that the Soviet Union and the US were edging towards a direct dialogue on Afghanistan instead of relying on other countries to bring them together.[15]

## REFERENCES

1. Cyrus Vance, 'Hard choice, critical year in *American Foreign Policy*, p. 391 cited in Dougles A. Borer, *Super Powers Defeated*, p. 185.
2. See Collins *The Soviet Invasion of Afghanistan*, p. 87 in Dougles A. Borer, op. cit., p. 185.
3. Galcotti, *Afghanistan*, pp. 17-18 cited in Dougles A. Borer, op. cit., p. 186.
4. Dougles A. Borer, op. cit., p. 186

5. Bhabani Sen Gupta, *The Afghan Syndrome, How to live with Soviet Power*, p. 11, see note on p. 252.

6. Ibid., p. 13. The official explanation of Soviet interest in Afghanistan appeared in *Pravada* 31 December 1979 and 24 January 1980.

7. Ibid.

8. *Times of India*, 30 December 1979 and 2 February 1980

9. Bhabani Sen Gupta, p. 16

10. Ibid.

11. *Hindu*, 20 January 1980

12. *Indian Express*, 1 February 1980 and also *Hindustan Times* of the same date

13. Bhabani Sen Gupta op. cit pp. 114-115.

14. Ibid., p. 129.

15. *Hindu*, 2 March 1980.

# 6

# Indira Gandhi's Come-back

In the general elections held in January 1980, Mrs. Gandhi's party came to power. This virtually coincided with the Soviet intervention in Afghanistan which had taken place in the last week of December 1979. This was the period of intense tension between the two super powers in which India's sympathy was regarded, in western circles, in favour of Moscow though the fact was that India had never approved of the Soviet intervention in Afghanistan. To ease the tension, New Delhi had repeatedly suggested to Washington to try to assess the compulsions under which Moscow had to intervene. This had no impact either on Carter or Reagan, the former took immediate steps to resume arms aid to Pakistan after modifying his much publicised decision in April 1979 to cut off all military and economic aid in the wake of the disclosure that Islamabad was pursuing a nuclear weapon programme.[1]

In taking this step, the American administration set aside India's contention that Pakistan was no threat from the Soviet side as the intervention in Afghanistan was a temporary measure and also that with the American arms aid, Pakistan wanted to achieve its traditional goal of military parity with India. President Carter wanted to sooth Indian sentiments and as a sop he authorised the shipment of 3.8 tons of enriched uranium for the Tarapur plant ignoring the Congressional opposition. To pursue the matter further India sent a delegation led by Homi Sethna, chairman of the Indian atomic energy commission in April 1981 but no concrete agreement could be reached because the issue of nuclear and arms aid to Pakistan came in the way.

The discussions on the US arms aid was again resumed when Mrs. Gandhi made use of her first-ever meeting with President Reagan on 21 October 1981 at Cancun. She forcefully repeated what had earlier been communicated to his administration with special reference to how Pakistan was exploiting the situation in Afghanistan to create tension in the wider region in South Asia. Reagan again put forth the old plea of American obligation towards its ally in view of the Soviet presence in Afghanistan. The meeting ended in a total failure as each party failed to convince the other of its viewpoint.[2]

In addition, two more decisions of the US government added to the strains in Indo-US relations. First, the US Senate, through an amendment to the foreign assistance act of 1980, voted on 22 October 1981 to cut off aid to India and Pakistan if either country detonated a nuclear device. Second, the US firmly stood against allocating a proposed International Monetary Fund (IMF) loan of $ 5.8 billion to India on the ground that the latter did not meet the Fund's policy conditions. However, the loan was approved on 10 November 1981 despite the US representative's negative vote.[3]

In the midst of growing strains in the relations of the two countries, Mrs. Gandhi accepted the invitation of President Reagan to visit the US. This she did in late July and early August 1982. The intractable problem apart, the two leaders seemed to have been talking at different wave lengths with the result that no worthwhile result could be achieved at these talks. On the issue of arms supply to Pakistan, the same old argument was repeated namely that Pakistan's defence capability required to be strengthened in view of the Soviet threat.

What could not be achieved in the form of concrete measures was sought to be done by expressing verbal pleasantries. The American leaders gave recognition to India's importance to the global strategy; they also claimed to share faith in human dignity and their allegiance to democratic values as a fact confirmed by history. The External Affairs Minister P.V. Narasimha Rao in a statement in the Parliament on 13 August 1982 stated that the US accepted India's role as a factor of 'stability and modernisation' in the Asian region, as well as in the broader international context.[4] Apparently all such statements were taken in India on their face value.

Mrs. Gandhi was more plain speaking in her utterances. She tried to clear the impression that India was pro-Soviet while dealing with the super powers. Referring to the Afghan crisis, she said India was opposed to any sort of intervention, 'military or political' in the internal affairs of any other nation. The Soviet Union should not be singled out for criticism on Afghan issue; she reminded that the US had also interfered in the affairs of certain developing countries. The visit of Mrs. Gandhi left all the old 'doubts', 'misunderstandings' and 'areas of disagreement' in tact. The one saving grace of the visit was that it brought about an agreement on the outstanding issue of nuclear fuel supply to the Tarapur plant. According to the agreement, France would replace the US as supplier of the much needed nuclear fuel to India. This could be possible only because the US agreed to it.

In the aftermath of Mrs. Gandhi's visit, the relations between the two countries continued to remain marked by frequent irritants. India repeated its resentment over American administration's decision in August 1982 to extend fresh credit for arms sales to Pakistan. The US expressed its unhappiness over Mrs. Gandhi's statement during her visit to Mauritius regarding Indian Ocean states' support for Mauritius's sovereignty over Diego Garcia.[5]

Mrs. Gandhi's visit to Moscow in September 1982 created some uneasiness in Washington. Her interactions with the Soviet leaders and the agreements envisaging defence and economic cooperation between India and the USSR further strengthened the American impression of India's pro-Soviet leanings. Equally disturbing to the US were the contents included in the joint communique issued at the end of Mrs. Gandhi's Moscow visit in which several references were made to the situation in Afghanistan, foreign bases in Indian Ocean and several other issues which were not palatable to the US administration.

## Schultz's Visit

The disparaging utterances made by the leaders of the two countries created misunderstanding on both sides to remove which personal contacts between the dignitaries of the two countries were considered necessary. The first attempt in that direction was made when the US administration decided to send its Secretary of State George Shultz to India in the last week of June 1983. He made a few statements before he left for India which were meant to suggest America's desire to improve relations with India; one of the steps they wanted to take was to supply safety related spare parts for the Tarapur atomic plant which could not be obtained elsewhere.[6]

During his visit Shultz was reported to have assured the Indian leaders that the US was prepared to sell sophisticated military equipment to India without too many conditions. But the Indian government did not agree to the proposal on the ground that apart from the high price factor involved there was no firm guarantee of an assured supply of essential spare parts and ammunition on the required scale under the existing US laws and procedures besides the known disinclination on the part of Washington to transfer advanced technology and let India manufacture such weaponry indigenously under licence.[7]

There was another serious reason attached to India's refusal. India did not want to get caught in this trap of indirectly justifying the US arms supplies to Pakistan by purchasing weaponry from the same source even if the equipment was sold without any stringent conditions. In order to stress India's contention that US arms supplies to both countries could create so many complexities that relations between the two countries would get irreparably damaged.

But for this issue, the extensive discussions that Shultz had with Mrs. Gandhi and P.V. Narasimha Rao were more in the nature of amicable conversation rather than serious discussion aimed at narrowing down the divergences of opinion. But the American guest continued to harp on American views of regarding India as a stable force to maintain peace in the subcontinent.

From the Indian point of view the Shultz visit had not held out any hope of change in the near future in the US policies of arming Pakistan even at the risk of starting a new arm race in the subcontinent. On other issues also, Shultz's response was not at all encouraging. The US had already opposed further flow of concessional financial assistance to India through multilateral channels like IDA; it had also stood in the way of the Indian request for two billion dollar loan from the Asian Development Bank and even denied transfer of technology for industrial purposes. He had no valid answer to give to these Indian grievances; all that he did was to listen intently, put some questions to seek more clarification from the Indian side and finally promised to convey his impressions to President Reagan on his return to Washington.

The only tangible outcome of Shultz's visit had been the understanding reached over the supply of spare parts for Tarapur plant but it was plagued by so many uncertainties that no one on the Indian or American side was prepared to hazard any guess as to how it was going to be settled, particularly in the face of growing Congressional opposition in Washington.

Shultz left on 2 July on his way to Pakistan; before leaving he described his trip as a very fine visit. P.V. Narasimha Rao said that wide ranging discussions with him were 'satisfactory and promising' to sustain the impression that despite persisting differences over several issues, the talks had helped to clear up some of the misgivings and doubts on either side.[8]

## II

As an effort to maintain regular contacts between the leaders of the two countries Mrs. Gandhi made it a point to hold talks with Reagan when she was in New York in September 1983 to address the 38th session of the UN General Assembly. The meeting took place on 26 September after Reagan had addressed the UN General Assembly session. He did not mention India specifically in his address but his reference to what he called pseudo-non alignment must have hurt Mrs. Gandhi. Since she was the chairperson of the non aligned movement he must have known that any unfavourable reference to it was bound to affect Indo-US relations.[9]

Another incident that marred the significance of this meeting was the growing conviction in official and non official American circles over India's reaction to the downing of a South Korean civilian airliner by the Soviet missile earlier in the month in international waters off Soviet Asia causing death of 269 innocent passengers. Critics reminded that it was like India's refusal to condemn the Soviet invasion of Hungary in 1956.[10] Although 44 nations had asked to address the Security Council during the debate on this issue, Indian representative did not care to speak. In general, Indian government's statement on the affair was called 'mealy mouthed' by the American officials. Still Reagan considered it important to lean over backwards to try to persuade the non aligned movement particularly its leader India to realise the heinous character of the tragedy and its implications on international relations.

Mrs. Gandhi's main mission was to conduct the deliberations of a mini-summit from 27 to 29 September which was attended by over 25 members. The non aligned conference held in New Delhi earlier in the year conceived the idea of a mini-summit during the 38th session of the UN

General Assembly. This became all the more relevant in the context of heightened international tension prevailing then following several international developments including the latest super power dispute over the Korean plane disaster.[11]

As a reaction to these developments, the Soviet Union decided, for the first time in 26 years, not to send its Foreign Minister Andrei Gromyko to attend the UN session. Most of the NAM countries viewed Gromyko's absence as an unfortunate development though they were wary of taking sides in the super power disputes. For India, it was significant as it was there that it was expected to be elected to the Security Council.

The success of Mrs. Gandhi's visit to the USA lay in another field. In spite of the virtual rebuff she received from most of the heads of state and government who did not attend the mini NAM summit the impression left behind by her was that she was not a leader who wilted under opposition attack. The US visit helped her to project the image of a strong and determined world leader able to hold her own in hostile conditions.[12]

As regards Indira Gandhi-Reagan talks, they were held without agenda; what was discussed was a general survey of international affairs in which the role of the NAM was assessed. Besides, they discussed the means by which global mistrust and suspicion could be removed and a climate conducive to bring about world peace be created. No contentious bilateral issue was taken up as it was neither the opportune movement to discuss it nor was there any need for reviewing issues which were frequently being discussed between the two sides ever since Mrs. Gandhi's last visit about a year ago.

The year 1984 was marked by certain irritants that gave a setback to the Indo-US relations. The US administration had agreed to supply spare parts for the Tarapur atomic plant but later it started showing reluctance to meet the entire requirements of spares because India by a bilateral arrangement with Germany got some spares but it had no bearing at all on the contractual obligations of the US to meet our requirements in terms of the 1963 agreement. Another controversy arose over the sale of a computer for Indian air lines service. India refused to accept the condition that it would have to seek prior permission for putting the computer to a different use even within the country. Another issue arose during the negotiations on signing bilateral memorandum of understanding (MOU) as an inter-governmental umbrella agreement to regulate the sale of military equipment by standardising the conditions, it had run into difficulties because the US continued to insist on retaining an overriding clause empowering it to cancel any agreement at any stage without assigning any reason.

To sum up, Indo-US relations during the second tenure of Mrs. Gandhi 1980-84 did not show much improvement. Though Mrs. Gandhi tried to create a rapport with the American leadership, the latter was firm in their commitment to Pakistan which was a factor that always came in the way of the two countries developing cordial relations. Even on personal level, at times, there was acrimony when the two sides were face to face to discuss some controversial issues. There was one more factor to be reckoned with. During the preceding period of Janata regime, Carter and Desai could develop personal rapport and though they differed on several issues bitterness did not mark the process of negotiations. But during Mrs. Gandhi's tenure, because of temperamental incompatibilities between the two sides, most of the bilateral issues were coloured by personal dispositions.

### Visit by Bush

The US Vice-President George Bush who was largely responsible for arranging Mrs. Gandhi's official visit in 1982 and ensuring the success of it, although the high expectations of renewal of warmth in Indo-US relations did not last long in the wake of other international developments, arrived here on a four-day visit on 13 May 1984. There was no body more influential and politically closer to the President than George Bush to provide a sweetner to the otherwise soured Indo-US relations. He came with a personal message from Reagan making the customary assurance of goodwill for India and renewed assertion that the limited arms supply to Pakistan would not have any effect on the security of India.

There was another favourable factor to give a good start to Indo-US relations. By the time of Bush's visit India's economic relations with the US had much improved particularly in the field of trade. The trade turnover in 1983, was over $4 billion with exports to the US touching $2.19 billion and imports from the US amounting to $1.82 billion leaving a marginal surplus of $37 million in India's favour. As regards US investments, the total value touching $ 500 million, the US had the highest foreign investments in the country after UK. Besides, of the 590 foreign collaboration proposals approved in 1982, 110 were with the US and that during the first half of 1982, 67 of the 350 collaboration proposals were with the US companies.[14]

Even before Bush arrived, it was decided in New Delhi that there would be no point in raising the old irritants like Tarapur spares because of America's unwillingness to pull its weight in the multilateral funding agencies. It was felt that India's views on these subjects were already well known in Washington. Moreover in matters regarding the US stance towards the World Bank and IMF, the US Treasury Department played the determining role and the Vice-President had other minor role to play. Instead, New Delhi treated the Bush visit for a free, frank and wide ranging discussions.

During the talks, Mrs. Gandhi sought Bush's assessment of the recent visit of President Reagan to China. He explained some of the Reagan's commitments to China made during his visit. The fact that Washington had offered nuclear collaboration to China in return for the guarantees which, for India, were found inadequate, only lent greater evidence to India's long standing charge that the nuclear non-proliferation regimes discriminated against nuclear non-weapon states.[15]

When his attention was drawn to the 'double standards' that the US had applied in not seeking from China the same sort of nuclear guarantees that it was demanding from India for the fulfillment of its contractual obligations in regard to the Tarapur plant, Bush merely said that he was satisfied that China would not use any nuclear equipment supplied by the US for enhancing its military potential. This he obviously said without going into the details of the understanding reached with Beijing.[16]

Bush sought to defuse Indian criticism by saying that India could acquire arms from the USA. But he should have known that India's desire to diversify its weapon purchase to the US had been thwarted by problems of technology transfer, the US insistence on the right to choke off the supply pipeline at any moment and exaggerated Pentagon fears over the risk of sophisticated American arms falling into Russian hands. Besides, the American arms were several times more expensive than the Russian variety. The US would supply arms to India at market rate whereas to Pakistan it gave at a throw away price.

Bush made no promises which his administration had no intention to live up to. He did not say that it would cut off military assistance to Pakistan in case Islamabad acquired nuclear weapons. All that he said was that the US had communicated to Pakistan its views on non-proliferation. Whether mere communication of views would serve any purpose was a doubtful proposition. Similarly he had not held out the assurance that his country would do all in its power to see to it that Pakistan did not use weapons supplied by it against India.[17] On the other hand he reminded that India was also purchasing arms from some other countries and that his government could not properly dictate to India that these weapons would be used only against a specific power. At the press conference he dismissed suggestion of a guarantee that the arms provided to Pakistan would not be turned against India pointing out that it would in any case be meaningless as experience in 1965 and 1971 had shown.[18]

**Murphy's Visit**

The US Assistant Secretary of State Richard Murphy arrived here on a 3-day visit on 20 October 1984 while on his way to Mauritius and North and South Yemen. He was considered an important dignitary in the State Department as he initiated most of the US policy decisions relating to India and Pakistan. His predecessor James Burckley was largely responsible for the US decision in 1981 to rearm Pakistan in a big way after the Soviet intervention in Afghanistan. Now when Murphy was in India, Burckley was on a private visit to Pakistan as a personal guest of Zia-ul Haq to revive his old contacts with him. He was reported to have said in Islamabad in the wake of the controversial speech of the American ambassador Dean Hinton that the US would not remain a silent spectator in the event of an attack on Pakistan, although he took care to stress that the US did not expect India to commit such an aggression.[19]

Murphy was regarded in India as the initiator of the new US moves to upgrade further the level of US arms supplies to Pakistan by including more sophisticated systems besides extending the military aid programme beyond 1980 after the present $ 3.2 billion package ran out. The government of India was keen to know whether in talking of the American commitment to defend Pakistan the US was trying to reactivate the 1981 mutual security pact with Pakistan. Murphy could not give any convincing explanation; what he did was only to repeat the bland assurance of the past that the US military aid to Pakistan was primarily meant for its defence against a possible Soviet attack through Afghanistan and that in speaking of the US commitments to defend Pakistan's territorial integrity, the Reagan administration was not perceiving any Indian threat to it.[20]

**After Mrs. Gandhi**

According to a Congressional analyst Richard Cronin, the Indian foreign policy during Mrs. Gandhi's period was not so much driven by some 'inexorable factors' as by her personal viewpoint bolstered by Soviet efforts to achieve certain objectives which were likely to clash with American interests. So there was a perceived need, felt in some American circles to prevent the Russians from winning over her successor, Rajiv Gandhi. Some powerful sections in the Pantagon were also thinking on these lines and planning to court India on Indian terms by, for instance, conceding the Indian demand for highly developed military items. The Assistant Secretary for Defence, Richard Armitage was sponsoring the idea that the obvious way to disengage India from the Soviet Union was to offer very high technological products which Moscow could not match.[21]

The visit of General A.S. Vaidya to the US in July was believed to have been encouraged by those who were pursuing this line of action. From the Indian side it was a step towards diversifying sources of armament supply which the US army high ups welcomed by showing him around to a variety of military goods of high order. He was also assured of their being supplied on reasonable terms and also of the regular supply of the spares. From the American side, the Defence Department dispatched Armitage's special assistant Ron Zward to the subcontinent to assess the situation and confer with government officials in New Delhi and Islamabad.

Mrs. Gandhi's death was received with great shock all over America; the good will and admiration for a sister democracy in bereavement was shown in many ways. American leaders and resident Indians joined together in a rally to pay homage to Mrs. Gandhi and deplore the violence which had killed her. The Congressmen, of both the parties reaffirmed their commitments to preserve the territorial integrity of India. Although the US Presidential election was just a few days away, India continued to attract the local media.

The US Secretary of State George Shultz led a high power delegation to attend Mrs. Gandhi's funeral. On arrival, he said in a statement, 'we shall do so as we did with the government of Rajiv Gandhi's great and distinguished mother to whom over thoughts turn so strongly, so warmly on this tragic day'. In another touching reference he said, 'I speak for all

Americans when I tell you how profoundly shocked we were by the brutal act of terrorism which has taken Indira Gandhi from us'.[22]

Later when Shultz met Rajiv Gandhi he held out the hope that the US administration would try to improve its relationship with India by striving for a better balance in its involvement in the subcontinent without in any way weakening its links with Pakistan. Rajiv reminded that India had at no stage suggested that the US should not have good relations with Pakistan but it had only been striving that the focus would shift from military aid to economic assistance. A stable and prosperous Pakistan would not pose a threat to India like a militarily strong but politically weak one bent on pursuing a confrontation policy to condition the psyche of its people with the bogey of an Indian threat.

On the re-election of Ronald Reagan as the US President, India looked forward to further strengthening the friendly ties between the two countries. Messages of congratulations to this effect were sent by both President Zail Singh and Prime Minister Rajiv Gandhi. The Americans had given the assurance but the Reagan government was not going to take any decisive steps till the outcome of the Parliamentary poll in India was known. Then alone, the US administration would be in a position to know what moves it should take to determine new tenor of Indo-US relations.

The congratulatory messages were scanned carefully in Washington and it was noted that no doubt, they indicated India's desire for better understanding with the US without giving any misleading impression that the new government in India was inclined to tilt towards Washington. It was quite in keeping with the spirit of American assurance conveyed by Shultz that in developing cordial relations with India they would not weaken their links with Pakistan.

Top American leaders appeared anxious to woo Rajiv and try to open a new and happier chapter in Indo-US relations. Subsequent to the visit of Shultz another dignitary to visit

India was Clairbon Pell, a ranking member of the Senate Foreign Relations Committee. He paid a tribute to the resilience of India's democratic system after Mrs. Gandhi's death which manifested itself in its capacity to produce a leader equal to his national task.[23]

In his report, Pell said that while Rajiv Gandhi did not signal any departure from India's traditional or foreign policy but he left the impression that once elected he would give many issues a fresh look. The period following the election would offer a great opportunity to improve Indo-US relations. He noted that Rajiv's education and personal orientation was distinctly western. Besides, his technological bent and his relatively non-ideological pragmatism were quite congenial to the American mind set.

A delegation of four Democratic Senators led by Sam Nunn arrived here on 29 December 1984. They came to India primarily at the suggestion of the US ambassador Hary Barnes who had been pressing them to visit the subcontinent to get a better idea of Indian policies and aspirations in the period immediately following the death of Mrs. Gandhi. The idea of this visit was mooted much before Mrs. Gandhi's assassination; it acquired significance during the turmoil that followed her death. Its itinerary was changed to suit Rajiv Gandhi's convenience as he was likely to be away from Delhi from 1 December on the election campaign. Earlier, the idea was to send Charles Percy, former chairman of the Senate Foreign Relations Committee to make a reappraisal of the prospects for closer Indo-US relations. But it was considered a better substitute to send a delegation of four Democratic Senators as their views would reflect wider spectrum of public opinion.

What was more important than the visit of this team of Senators to the subcontinent was the impending trip to Pakistan by the Chairman of the US Joint Chiefs of Staff Gen. John Vassey, the highest ranking American military officer to make an on the spot assessment of Pakistan's additional military assistance request for the supply of more sophisticated arms. One of the Senators visiting the subcontinent Sam Nunn who was Chairman of the Senate Armed Services Committee would join the army chief along with John Glenn, a ranking member of the Senate Foreign Relation Committee.[24]

Another important American dignitary who came to meet Rajiv Gandhi was the Republican Senator Larry Pressler, the author of the amendment which laid down the conditions on the fulfilment of which supply of nuclear material to India and Pakistan could be permissible. He was told clearly by Rajiv that the US tilt towards Pakistan was the main stumbling block in Indo-US relations. Pressler retorted that India's attitude towards the Soviet Union was another stumbling block. He believed that the US was losing India to the Soviet Union and he did not think much could be done to rectify the situation; he wanted India to be a reliable neutral. Pressler categorically asserted that the US would not only maintain its supply of arms to Pakistan at the existing level but would increase it if the Soviet Union stepped up its strength in Afghanistan. As regards the working of the new government Pressler believed that there was no concrete evidence of Rajiv Gandhi breaking new ground in India's relations towards the US but he hoped that Gandhi would shed some of the old rhetorics. He called it an absolutely baseless allegation that the CIA was working to destabilise India or of its involvement in the assassination of Mrs. Gandhi.

## REFERENCES

1. P. Sahadevan, op. cit, p. 531
2. *Statesman*, 23 October 1981
3. P. Sahadevan, op. cit., p. 533
4. *Indian Express*, 14 August 1982
5. P. Sahadevan, op cit., p. 536.
6. *Asian Recorder*, 6-12 August 1983, p. 17302

7. Ibid.

8. Ibid.

9. K.R. Sunder Rajan in the *Tribune*, 10 October 1983.

10. Soi Saunders in the *Indian Express*, 20 September 1983

11. R. Chakrapani in the *Hindu*, 23 September 1983

12. *Tribune*, 4 October 1983 edit. 'Mixed Balance Sheet'

13. See P. Sahadevan p. 538 and *Hindu*, 12 January 1984

14. *Hindustan Times,* 12 May 1984

15. N.C. Menon in *Hindustan Times*, 16 May 1984

16. *Hindu*, 16 May 1984 from G.K. Reddy

17. *Times of India*, 16 May 1984, edit: 'False Promises'

18. *Hindu*, 17 May 1984 edit: 'Mr. Bush's Visit'.

19. *Hindu*, 22 October 1984 from G.K. Reddy

20. Ibid

21. Bharat Karnard in *Hindustan Times*, 16 November 1984

22. *Hindustan Times*, 3 November 1984

23. *Statesman*, 20 November 1984

24. *Hindu,* 24 November 1984, from G.K. Reddy.

# 7

# Rajiv Gandhi in Office

After the assassination of Mrs. Gandhi on 30 October 1984, Rajiv Gandhi assumed Prime Minister's office as leader of the Congress Party. Much optimism greeted in the US the advent of his regime for the fact that by upbringing and education he had developed pro-western orientation in his out look and being a man of technological set of mind he was a forward looking statesman. A number of American dignitaries who had met him earlier felt that he would be more friendly to the West than his mother was.

The one handicap from which Mrs. Gandhi suffered was that she, while being in the company of her father, for over a major part of her impressionable life, had witnessed some of the indiscreet acts, committed, from time to time, by the US administration in belittling the status and importance of India and questioning its bonafides on various steps that it had to take to safeguard its national interests. This left a scar of bitterness on her mind which she could not easily efface. The memory of the role played by Nixon administration during the Bangladesh crisis was too fresh to be easily forgotten.

Rajiv Gandhi was to a great extent free from such obsessions; what he saw and heard about political affairs was a mere second-hand information to which he gave a passing attention. Most of the time he was busy in his professional assignments and looking after his family affairs to which, Mrs. Gandhi even being the head of an Indian family, could not spare much time. Besides, he had built up a circle of friends who were more or less apolitical. Sudden emergence as the leader of a big power changed the entire scenario in which he found himself face to face with problems which were simply overwhelming.

President Reagan was keen to develop fresh relations with Rajiv in order to give a new twist to the Indo-US relations. When he came to know that Rajiv Gandhi had accepted his invitation to visit the US, he regarded this as the most important event during his second term. The importance that the public opinion attached to this event was reflected in the unanimous resolution that both the Houses of the Congress had passed welcoming the visit of Rajiv Gandhi to their country.

## Rajiv Gandhi's Visit—I

Rajiv Gandhi reached Washington on 12 June 1985 on a five-day visit. President Reagan, in welcoming him, likened the visit to the 'voyage of discovery' made by Jawaharlal Nehru in 1949. Reagan assured Rajiv that he would discover that the US remained steadfastly dedicated to India's unity and that they were firmly opposed to those who tried to undermine it. This statement was made in the background of a few sikhs shouting anti-Indian slogans in a park nearby.

Realistically speaking, the Rajiv–Reagan talks that followed soon after his arrival, were looked upon as a get-acquainted meeting with each other trying to probe the mind of the other to assess what pattern of relations could be expected in the future. An official spokesman was quite candid in stating that the US did not look upon the visit as a 'break through' visit, or one from which 'dramatic new departures' from the existing relationship could be expected. They admitted that there had been differences between the two countries and they would continue to persist. In Rajiv's visit they got an opportunity to get to know how he viewed India's future and where the US could fit in.

The meeting was arranged in such a way that more time was set apart for private discussions with the President and his cabinet colleagues. On 12 June he had two prolonged sessions with Reagan and a meeting with Secretary of State George Shultz. He also met groups of Congressmen of both the parties. The programme included his meetings with the American scientists and corporate executives. There were reports that the US was seeking an entry in the Indian market to join some of the western states in meeting some of India's defence needs. There was a possibility of American contribution to India's efforts in the area of indigenous production of defence items. The American spokesman observed that they were interested in responding to India's desire to diversify its source of supply and to increase its independence in the defence field.[1]

Later it was discovered that there was not much interest on the question of Indian purchases of defence items. The Prime Minister himself had said, 'we have not discussed this in any great depth'. Even the American official spokesman, Barnard Kalb discouraged speculation about the arms deal. In his view, the Indians were not on a shopping visit, nor were the Americans going to push such sales. There was some discussion on arms sale but this was not the central issue.[2]

It was because some of the sales conditions were not acceptable to India, one of them being that the terms of supply could be altered retroactively by the US. Secondly, there were doubts about the reliability of the US as a supplier of spare parts and other equipments. Apart from direct sale, the US concluded an agreement with India on transfer of high technology which would enable it to import technology for agriculture and industry as well as military purposes. It had also expressed its readiness to consider specific military technology areas in which India may be interested. The underlying US strategy was to reduce Soviet predominance in the sale of military items to India. But India had to consider all implications before deciding to include the US in its policy of diversification as regards military purchases.

Rajiv Gandhi had, on several occasions during the talks with the US leaders, brought in the question of continued US arms supplies to Pakistan in the face of the latter's efforts to make a nuclear bomb. This posed a double danger to India the consequences of which would be incalculably high. The public opinion in the country on this issue was very restive and there were growing pressures within the country that India must go nuclear before the danger looms large on our door steps.

The Defence Secretary Weinberger tried to assure Gandhi that even though the Reagan administration had in its budget estimates for 1987-88 earmarked some additional military aid for Pakistan (beyond the $ 3.2 billion package) it had made no open-ended commitment to Islamabad and that if the situation in South Asia were to improve there need not be any continuation of arms supplies to Pakistan. Reagan also gave a similar assurance to Rajiv and hoped that India's active role in Afghanistan could change this situation. This was too far fetched a view which did not carry much weight with him. Nor had they any satisfactory response to Rajiv Gandhi's contention that the US arms supplied to Pakistani could not be used in the mountainous region of Afghanistan; they were suitable only for the Indian terrain.[3]

However, he left Americans in no doubt that if and when the government of India came to know from its own intelligence sources that Pakistan had detonated a nuclear device or that it had a bomb in the basement, the Indian response could be short and swift. Rajiv informed them that the Indian intelligence reports showed that Pakistan was very close to making the bomb. According to a senior officer, who was connected with the discussions, India's concern had never been conveyed so explictely at the highest level.[4] The American response was that they would intensify their pressure on Pakistan and they would also expect India stepping up its bilateral efforts to normalise its relations with Pakistan.

As regards the Afghan crisis, since January 1985, the Reagan administration had been suggesting to India that it should get more active in pursuing a political settlement in Afghanistan. During his visit to Moscow in May 1985 it seemed that Rajiv Gandhi made some suggestions to Gorbachev on this issue and the Soviet leader was believed to have responded positively. The Prime Minister came back with the impression that Moscow would be willing to pull out of Afghanistan provided the USA took some corresponding steps to ensure Afghanistan's sovereignty, integrity and non aligned status and safe return of the refugees to their homeland.

This message Rajiv Gandhi conveyed to Reagan and sought the latter's reactions. According to the press reports, the US response was also encouraging. After consultation with his top advisers Gandhi evaluated the US suggestions and decided to ask the Foreign Secretary, Romesh Bhandari to go to Moscow to convey to the Soviet leaders the US response. If this mission succeeded the US-Soviet talks scheduled to be held in Washington on some technical aspects of the Afghan problems were likely to be influenced. And if the two super powers showed a genuine desire to work for a political settlement, there was a chance that India might step in and reinforce UN Secretary General's initiative. Rajiv Gandhi realised the limitations of his country to launch on this adventure, so he was very cautious to make any more move in this direction.

One important event of the visit which was not highlighted by the press was the call on Gandhi by the well known scientist Carl Segam who was vigorously campaigning for an end of the nuclear race. He had propounded a theory with which even a Pentagon appointed group had concurred. It was the possibility of a 'nuclear winter' which would shut out the sun and thereby lead to sub-zero temperature on the earth resulting in an end to life and vegetation. The main purpose of the astronomer's visit was to present to the Indian Prime Minister a statement signed about 80 Nobel prize winners and others appealing a call by Indian Prime Minister and five other nations for a halt for the testing and production of nuclear weapons.[5]

The joint statement issued at the end of Rajiv Gandhi's visit contained no mention of a couple of issues about which the two countries remained worried: a potential nuclear arms race in the subcontinent and Afghanistan. On the first issue, India was reported to have clearly pointed its finger to Pakistan as a major source of proliferation threat to the whole region. The Reagan administration, on the other hand, was reportedly content to refer in general terms to South Asia being in imminent danger of nuclear proliferation which apparently included India also. As for Afghanistan, Washington had hoped for some modification which did not materialise, in India's 'strongly held view equating Soviet 'intervention' in that country with 'interference' in the form of external assistance from across the Pakistan border to the Afghan Mujahedeens.[6]

The views in both cases were so divergent that the two sides decided to drop the topics from the communique altogether rather than risk harming the promising climate in Indo-US relations. The joint statement therefore referred only to the fact that the two leaders reviewed the situation in the South Asian region by expressing their respective views about the regional security environment. This included, by implications the threat of nuclear proliferation, arms to Pakistan and the crisis in Afghanistan, the subjects in which India was particularly interested. They were not mentioned by name as then alone the two sides could sign the document without reservations.

The statement noted with concern the emergence of organised terrorism as a threat to peace and democracy and urged all governments to take appropriate steps to combat this new danger. The document further hoped close cooperation and consultation on the international dimensions of terrorist violence against India. This clearly referred to the terroristic activities aided by Pakistan in the state of Kashmir. On this score, the US side did not embarrass the Indian delegation by including Palestinian Liberation Organisation (PLO) as a terrorist body. The US official policies regarded PLO as the prime international terrorist organisation.

In concrete terms, the outcome of Rajiv Gandhi-Reagan talks was the enunciation of new initiatives announced by President Reagan himself in his farewell speech on 20 October 1987. Briefly stated they were as follows: i) extension of three-year Indo-US initiative on science and technology; (ii) expansion in bilateral trade and reduction in trade barriers and check on 'protectionism; (iii) cooperation in India's need for upgraded technology dealing with computer science; (iv) pledging cooperation in stemming drug trafficking; (v) expansion in defence cooperation with special reference to LCA; (vi) enhancement in the productivity in arid zone agriculture and water management; (vii) utilization of Indo-US fund for cultural and scientific cooperation (viii) planning exchange of visits by dignitaries and parliamentarians of the two countries; (ix) commencing a programme for fellowship in research institutes of science and technology.[7]

One beneficial outcome of Rajiv Gandhi's visit was the decision of Washington to provide high technology to India in a variety of fields including the strategic areas of defence. The transfer of such technology had vast potential for a great leap effect on the Indian economy. The agreement reflected a stage in evolution in Indo-US relations. So far the administration for, strategic reasons, had placed severe restrictions on the transfer of technology which made collaboration with India well nigh impossible. The obvious fear, on the part of Americans was that the know how would leak to the Soviet Union or its allies.

The US had high expectations of hi-tech trade with India. That was the reason why Washington opted to get a Memorandum of Understanding out of the way before Rajiv's visit. The MOU provided assurances against diversion of American hi-technology from the specific projects for which it was extended. India already had a credible reputation in the maintenance of confidentiality, the assurances in the MOU merely formalised the belief and faith on both sides. Moreover, the basic infrastructure for such an effort to succeed already existed as did other opportunities for interaction between the corporate sector of the two countries. However, it reflected Washington's new found confidence in India's potential as a trading and industrial partner that it planned to send out later exploratory teams in the fields of telecommunication and electronics in which India had a substantial modern sector.

What was the US objective in developing scientific relations with India. It was partly because Washington was convinced that greater scientific and technological collaboration and increased trade would bring about changes in India resulting in the more balanced form of non alignment. The US understood India's commitment to non alignment and had no quarrel with that. But Washington's efforts to interact more with India were based upon the hope that a more 'balanced' India's posture between East and West was a reasonable and realistic long term project.[8]

Even before the visit took place, the US government had privately cautioned both in Delhi and Washington against any excessive expectations of a spectacular upsurge in Indo-US relations as a result of Rajiv Gandhi's visit since the persisting differences over many issues could not be sorted out merely by a short visit of the dignitary of one country to the other. The main emphasis was on removing the avoidable strains through a frank exchange of views on each other's concerns and compulsions.

There was a clear indication that the US arms policy towards Pakistan would not undergo any change. The six-year $3.2 billion military supply programme ending in 1987, would continue beyond that period. The agreement provided for continuing the military sales programme and conferred the right on Pakistan to purchase arms on a cash basis after the expiry of the accord. The arms programme that was in operation had a salutary effect on the US relations with Pakistan though a price had to be paid on this score in the form of straining its ties with India. The arms supply relationship which was in a state of atrophy was revived in 1981 and began to strengthen Pakistan's capacity to deal with the Soviet threat arising from its presence in Afghanistan. The American argument was two fold, the US arms supply would not disturb the given disparity in the military power as between India and Pakistan, so it would not affect India's interest. Secondly, the American arms supply to Pakistan would not be directed against India. The arms supply to Pakistan was meant to strengthen Pakistan's defence capability on its western frontier rather than the Indian border particularly. As a rejoinder the Indian objection was that some of the highly sophisticated equipments sought by the Zia regime like the Haw Kaye airborne radar system, the Harpoon missiles, the Mohawk battlefield surveillance aircraft, the Vulcan Phalanse air defence equipment, the improved tow missiles for anti-tank warfare, and the updated offensive capabilities of F-16 aircraft could be used only against it in the sub-continental terrain.

From the US point of view the principal outcome of the visit was that some sort of rapport was established between the top American leadership on one hand and Rajiv Gandhi on the other for a cooperative and sympathetic personal relationship. The Americans found Rajiv Gandhi and his colleagues the kind of people with whom they could conduct frank and honest discussions expressing both agreements and disagreements without rancour. The US realised that if the two countries were to have a growing relationship capable of maturing into a series of mutual understandings the capacity for an open sympathetic discussion among the leaders was indispensable.

**Rajiv Gandhi's Visit—II**

Fears were expressed in India that the US or at least a section of its intelligence apparatus was out to destabililse the country by encouraging secessionist forces in various parts of the country particularly in Punjab. This was apparent from what often happened in the Congress. In June 1987, a debate took place in the House of Representatives in which 8 Congressmen belonging to the Republican party and the other seven to the Democratic party took part. Many of them showed little understanding or knowledge of the issues involved in the Punjab situation and voiced criticism of the Indian government.[9]

They were clearly told by the Indian spokesmen that they had not cared to see the unfortunate events in Punjab in correct perspective. The primary issue there was terrorism. They were supported with clippings of foreign press coverage of the events in Punjab with most of the stories emanating from different towns in the state. They were told to recall the days when the US was also faced with the spectrum of secession for which they had to pay a heavy price. In Punjab, a small faction of the Sikh community sought to impose its will over the rest by force. That could not be allowed.[10]

A section of US Congressmen interpreted the violence that broke out after Mrs. Gandhi's assassination as religious and ethnic outburst and 17 of them wrote on 5 August 1987 a letter to their ambassador to the UN to raise this issue before the UN Human Rights Commission at its next meeting. The Congressmen said, they were concerned about the violation of those human rights which the Indian Constitution had provided as inalienable rights. The question was raised in the Parliament on 25 August where it was called a 'disquieting development' amounting to interfering in our internal affairs.

In the US, President Reagan tended to have developed a tunnel vision about the threat of expanding Soviet influence in India. His concept of American policies towards the Indian subcontinent was mostly determined by his pre-conceived notion about Moscow's intentions. That was the reason why India failed to figure as a sizeable factor in America's strategic designs.[11] So, the Americans said, the main obstacle to desirable state of affairs had been their perception of an India unjustifiably and unwisely tilting towards Moscow.

In some American political circles it was felt that there was a calculated move in New Delhi to hound out friends of America both from the bureaucracy and from the Prime Minister's inner circle and they were being replaced by pro-Soviet elements. As an example it was stated that the exit of P.C. Alexander, as principal adviser to the Prime Minister, was the handiwork of pro-Soviet elements who were out to influence the new young Prime Minister. The immediate effect of this change was a sudden fall in Rajiv Gandhi's popularity and standing.[12]

When Rajiv Gandhi succeeded his mother as Prime Minister, there was much enthusiasm in the US coupled with the genuine hope that the needless misunderstanding between the two countries would soon be out of their way and a new relationship would develop. To bring about such a happy situation, Rajiv Gandhi decided to visit Washington on his way back from Vancouver (Canada) conference of Commonwealth Prime Ministers.

Before reaching Washington, Rajiv Gandhi made some statements which were meant to create a favourable environment for the forthcoming talks. In a session with the Indian journalists he expressed his personal praise for President Reagan. He laid the blame for increasing Indo-American differences, specifically regarding the US military build up of Pakistan on Reagan's aides particularly those in the Pentagon. Likewise, Rajiv Gandhi welcomed temporary suspension of US aid to Pakistan as a step forward and expressed the view that it should at least be tied positively with closing down of that country's nuclear programme. He said he would raise this question during his talks with Reagan and tell him what India had done to gain the friendship of Pakistan.

The US had also taken some steps which would evoke favourable reactions in India. For instance, defence was one of the new areas added to the US-India agenda in 1985 when some of the important developments had taken place. The US had approved the sale of an advanced jet fighter engine which was used in its F-18 Hornet while developing India's light combat aircraft. In September the US issued an export licence enabling India to acquire a powerful IMB computer with appropriate software for the defence and manufacture of the LCA. Other projects involving American components included a new gas turbine engine for Indian destroyers and specialized radars for other uses.[13]

Rajiv Gandhi made a one-day stop-over in Washington on 20 October, the last visit took place two years ago in June 1985. In order to reach Washington for this meeting with President Reagan, he had to cancel his visit to Ottawa to discuss bilateral Indo-Canadian issues with the Canadian Premier. As it was a non-State visit, it provided an opportunity to the Prime Minister to convey personally his views on issues which were blocking the way of smooth relationship of the two countries. As Rajiv had clearly stated that his main object in meeting Reagan would be to tell him to realise how dangerous situation, American supply of arms to Pakistan was creating in South Asia. He also pleaded with his American hosts not to provide Pakistan with an aerial early warning system which would not be useful on the Afghan border as proposed but as an offensive weapon against Indian border.

The two important callers on Rajiv Gandhi were, the acting Secretary of State John G. Whitehead; the Secretary of State Shultz was on a tour of West Asia on his way to Moscow, and Frank Carlucci, assistant to the President for national security affairs. He told both of them that Pakistan was engaged in a 'clandestine' programme to build a nuclear weapon which it concealed because it was controlled by its military. India, by contrast, conducted its nuclear programme in the open, under civilian operation and devoted to peaceful power production.

In this context an incident that occurred with Michael Armscost, the US Under Secretary of State for Political

Affairs may be stated to serve as a warning to the State officials. During his trip to Pakistan a few months ago, Armscost, it was reported, promised to keep the most recent exposure of Pakistani's surreptitious nuclear equipment acquisitions at a 'low key' if Islamabad merely would allow him to have a reassuring look at its Kohuta nuclear enrichment centre. Armscost's offer to temporize was given an abrupt 'no'. He felt much humiliated and beat a hasty retreat.[14]

After the two-hour meeting, both Indian Prime Minister and American President expressed satisfaction of what they had discussed and agreed to do. But the working paper published for the first time made no mention of the 'new initiative in Indo-US relations' which included 'defence cooperation' also. It included at least three items of US military equipment: *(a)* the air combat maneouvering range, a ground based system in which pilots simulate bombing targets and then grade them on their accuracy. This was something India had long been interested in acquiring to improve its training programme but up to now, the US navy had stood in opposition. *(b)* a missile range instrumentation system, similar to the USA's own set up at cape Canaveral for tracking missile test by telemetry and *(c)* an anti-tank missile.[15]

There were also discussions on joint Indo-US efforts to bring the Arjun tanks to the finishing stage and also working out cooperation on the already approved US General Electric engines for India's light combat aircraft. Rajiv Gandhi also received long-awaited assurance that India would get super computer for its weather reconnoitering. The White House was careful to state that the two governments would consult regularly to ensure that the US super computer exports reflected the rapid pace of advancing technology in India and that whatever India needed was to upgrade its capability.

India and USA disagreed on Afghan crisis. The government of India thought that the Najibullah regime in Kabul enjoyed wide support and would remain stable even after withdrawal of Soviet troops. The US administration disagreed. The Indian government gave legitimacy to the Kabul government by extending medical aid, by establishing with it a full diplomatic relationship and by inviting the Afghan premier Najibullah to visit New Delhi. The US administration did not agree with these presumptions and considered the Soviet-backed regime in Kabul not a legitimate government.

A vital difference between the approach of the two countries was with regard to the likely emergence of Islamic fundamentalism in Afghanistan after Soviet withdrawal. India viewed a serious danger in this menace but realised that being under the influence of a powerful communist state, the Afghan people would be more interested in exercising their right to self-determination not in the name of religion which was in a wrong way being practised as a state religion but out of their consideration to solve their economic problems. The US held a different view. In Iran where the principle of self-determination had been fully exercised and Ayatollah Khomeini enjoyed massive support, the US was opposed to it on grounds of its being a fundamentalist governed state. The American perception was that it was going to be a replica of the Khomeini type of fundamentalism in Afghanistan.

As regards the achievements of Rajiv Gandhi's visit it revealed a type of realism that would henceforth govern the relations of the two countries. It did not mean that the irritants of the sort that had so far affected the mutual ties disappeared or that the two countries would have no reason to complain against each other's attitudes on important issues. But it did mean that the two countries would not be deflected from the course of cooperation, in various spheres, that they had laid down two years ago during the first visit of Rajiv Gandhi.[16]

On one crucial issue, arms aid to Pakistan there was no illusion in India. The US decision was that it had to choose between its nuclear non-proliferation goals and its compulsions to use Pakistan as a convenient conduit to pump arms to the Mujahaddin rebels in Afghanistan. Washington was also well aware of Islamabad's determination to have a nuclear weapon option. Washington had to select one or the other but its efforts to have both created queer situation. Gandhi could not change Reagan administration's mind in this regard. The best Reagan could do was to echo Gandhi's concern about the dangers of nuclear spread, express the hope that nuclear competition in the region would be avoided and urge India and Pakistan to intensify their dialogue to resolve outstanding issues and to deal with the threat of nuclear proliferation in the region. The administration did not deviate from its long standing practice of equating India with Pakistan. The Prime Minister was successful in persuading the US Congress to view more cautiously the arms aid to Pakistan. His efforts made it far more difficult for Pakistan to obtain resumption of US aid which was cut off by the Congress on 30 September because the administration could not provide the assurance that Islamabad was not developing nuclear weapons.

Besides these issues, there were some other international developments that came in the way which caused irritation and tension. India criticised US military action against Libya and the External Affairs Minister, B.R. Bhagat visited Tripoli to express solidarity with the Libyan leaders. Washington expressed its annoyance by saying that the US cooperation in helping India to tackle the problem of terrorism would be conditional.[17] Another incident was related to Nicargua where American intervention was viewed by several other states as unjustified. On 22 October 1986 India's representative in the UN joined other members of the Security Council in seeking cessation of American intervention and intimidation against Nicargua[18] Also India played a leading role on 11 March 1987 at the UN Human Rights Commission in blocking an attempt by the US to subject Cuba to special scrutiny for alleged absence of fundamental rights. When the Commission endorsed the Indian mission proposal to shelve the US resolution expressing deep concern over alleged human rights violations and calling on Cuba to release all political prisoners, the US administration blamed India for causing such an embarrassing situation.[19]

## REFERENCES

1. *Hindu*, 6 June 1985 from R. Chakrapani
2. *Hindu*, 15 June 1985
3. J.N. Parimoo in *Times of India*, 22 June 1984
4. Ibid
5. *Hindu*, 15 June 1985 from R. Chakrapani
6. *Hindustan Times*, 14 June 1985 from Bharat Karnard
7. *Economic Times*, 25 October 1987
8. Ibid., 27 June 1985 from N.C. Menon in Washington
9. *Hindustan Times*, 13 July 1987
10. Ibid.
11. *Hindustan Times*, 20 August 1987 from N.C. Menon in Washington
12. Ibid
13. The US ambassador J. Dean's statement reported in *Times of India*, 10 October 1987
14. *Statesman*, 22 October 1987 from Warren Vnna
15. Ibid
16. K.K. Katyal in the *Hindu*, 26 October 1987
17. Statement by the US ambassador to the UN Vernon Walters *Tribune*, 28 April 1986
18. *Patriot*, 24 October 1986
19. *Telegraph, 15* March 1987

# 8

# The Pakistan Factor

Ever since the advent of cold war when the US had adopted the policy of containment by having a ring of multilateral defence pacts with the countries around the Soviet Union, Pakistan had been an ardent ally of the US. It was Pakistan that offered airbases and electronic monitoring stations on its territory from where American planes could make regular reconnaissance flights for spying purposes. There were various other gestures of helpfulness which convinced Washington that the security of Pakistan would ensure protection of US interests in South Asia. The US was not an Asian power as its arch rivals Soviet Union and China were. Pakistan made up that inadequacy by joining the US sponsored alliances in different regions.

India viewed these developments with much concern; it was feared that such a policy as was being followed by Pakistan at the instance of the US was bound to create tension which ultimately may lead to a conflict. India chose to stay away from such alliances. This was the main reason which annoyed the US and prompted by the feelings of animus Washington followed a policy biased against India. One concrete benefit that Pakistan got from following the US-led policy of alliances was the American arms aid ostensibly to safeguard the territorial integrity of Pakistan against any offensive from the Soviet side.

In the wake of Indo-Pak war in 1965 the US imposed an arms embargo on Pakistan probably because of the dismal performance by the Pak troops with the American weapons. This aroused much resentment even among those Congressmen who had earlier supported the arms deal in favour of Pakistan. During the Bangladesh war, the role played by Pakistan's army dictator Yahya Khan in getting Washington and Peking closer, Nixon administration in February 1972 decided to ease the embargo enabling Pakistan to make up the loss it had suffered during the war.

The resumption of arms aid in 1973 on the ground that the Soviet Union had been a major supplier of arms to India, Nixon contended that India's superiority in arms was so enormous that the possibility of Pakistan being a threat was absurd.[1] According to Kissinger it was largely the Indian factor which played the dominant role in shaping the US administration's decision to go to help Pakistan. He said, 'maintaining an embargo against a friendly country (Pakistan) while its neighbour (India) was producing and acquiring nearly a billion dollar worth of arms a year, was morally, politically and symbolically improper'.[2]

The US Secretary of State William Rogers told newsmen in New Delhi on 20 April 1973 that the arms issue was 'grossly exaggerated' as the United States supplies since 1965 amounted to a total of $100 million and included small quantities of spare parts and 300 armoured personnel carriers. He further clarified that the US had not supplied lethal arms to Pakistan. India, on the other hand, got supplies eight times more from the Soviet Union than what the US gave to Pakistan. Even France and Britain had supplied much larger quantities to India. Roger failed to tell that China also was a liberal supplier of arms to Pakistan and also that India had been buying arms by paying the full price while Pakistan was getting most of the arms as gift from the US.[3]

In an official publication of the State Department on arms embargo it was noted that India had received $ 1,697 million worth of arms between 1964 and 1973 and Pakistan just half of this, $ 851 million. It also showed that of its total imports India had received $ 1273 million in arms from the Soviet Union, $ 125 million from Czechoslovakia, $ 80 million from Britain, $ 88 million from the US and $ 48 million from France. By contrast, Pakistan had received $ 312 million in arms during the 10 year period from China, $ 214 million from France, $ 160 million from the US, $ 24 million from the Soviet Union and $ 8 million from Britain.[4]

However, Indian opposition to the resumption of arms supplies to Pakistan made Americans conscious of its negative effect on Indo-US relations. The American ambassador P. Moynihan assured Mrs. Gandhi on 15 March 1973 that the US would not supply any more lethal arms to countries on the Indian subcontinent, primarily Pakistan.[5] Henry Kissinger also assured the Senate Foreign Relations Committee on 11 September 1973 that the US would not be the 'principal' arms supplier to the Indian subcontinent in future. He went to the extent of saying that if a war broke out in that area it would not be because of American arms.[6]

These statements were very reassuring in that Bhutto who had been to the United States in September 1973 had assiduously tried to persuade the American leadership to adopt the policy of arms parity between India and Pakistan. But he failed to cut any ice with them. Henry Kissinger had personally assured Swaran Singh that the US always recognised that India's defence requirements were of much higher order as compared with those of Pakistan and that the US never supported the concept that the military strength of the two countries should be equal.[7]

Probably to sooth Indian sentiments, the US in 1973 agreed to release $ 87.6 million development aid to India which remained suspended since 1971. The other measure was the conclusion of an agreement on the settlement of the rupee accumulation arising from the PL 480 wheat sales to India.[8] But these were not very significant steps which would in any way neutralise India's resentment against US efforts to strengthen the belligerent capability of Pakistan.

India sharply reacted to the lifting of the US embargo as it would reopen the 'wounds' and 'hinder' the process of normalisation of relations between India and Pakistan. It was indeed strange that India's attempts to achieve self reliance in defence industry and its peaceful nuclear explosion were being trotted out as excuses for the American decision.[9] The real problem was that the US was still subscribing to the policy of equating India with Pakistan, a policy which had been the source of causing tension in the subcontinent.

It was also difficult to understand why the US was in such a hurry as to take this decision a little before the External Affairs Minister, Y.B. Chavan was to reach the US in March 1975. In response to an unanimous demand in Parliament he cancelled his visit. He warned the US Secretary of State, Henry Kissinger that the lifting of embargo would upset the recent trends of improvement in Indo-US relations and also hamper the process of normalisation of relations in the subcontinent.[10]

During the 1970s Indo-US relations remained at a low level but the assumption of Presidential office by Jimmy Carter which coincided with the Morarji Desai's Janta Party coming to power in New Delhi witnessed a change for the better. It had been a practice with the occupants of White House in Washington not to miss Pakistan while on a visit to India. But in July 1977 when Warren Christopher, the Deputy Secretary of State visited India, he did not include Pakistan in his itinerary. Similarly neither did Carter couple his visit to India in January 1978 with Pakistan.

A significant step that Carter took was to disapprove the sale of US-made A-7 fighter to Pakistan even though the outgoing Ford administration had approved the sale justifying it by saying that this would keep Pakistan army from developing nuclear capability. In early 1979 when US intelligence had gathered sufficient evidence about Islamabad's nuclear programme, the Carter administration invoked the Symington amendment under which Pakistan was barred from economic assistance.[11]

In dealing with matters of arms supplies to India and Pakistan even Carter administration could not dare to reverse his predecessor's policies. In 1977 the US administration disapproved sale to India of the Swedish made a deep penetration strike aircraft called SAAB-Viggen because a major part of its vital machine was solely prepared by the General Electric Company of America. India could do without it and preferred to go in for the Jagaur strike aircraft manufactured by British Aerospace.[12]

The Soviet intervention in Afghanistan in December 1979 changed the whole scenario. The day this event took place, Carter peremptorily revived the 1959 security commitment to Pakistan. The symington amendment was lifted to resume arms aid to Pakistan. Pakistan's nuclear development programme was overlooked as a secondary issue in the face of grave danger that the Soviet intervention in Afghanistan had posed to the security of Pakistan. A high power delegation led by Carter's national security adviser Brzezinski was sent to Pakistan to assess its arms requirements. Carter also sent his special emissary Clark Clifford to visit India to allay the Indian fears of resumption of military aid to Pakistan.

During the Afghan crisis, Pakistan was declared a 'front-line state' deserving the latest sophisticated weapons from the US. On 15 June 1981, Under Secretary of State James Buckley reached agreement in Islamabad on a $2.5 billion economic and military aid programme to Pakistan. It was not the amount of the deal that was of much concern to India but the type of weaponry that Pak got. This included the controversial sale of F 16 multi role fighter then among the most advanced fighters, previously supplied only to Egypt and Israel outside NATO. Not only was the F 16 superior to any thing that the IAF then possessed it also marked the first ever introduction of a multi role air craft capable of delivering nuclear weapons with a strike range that went beyond New Delhi.[13]

This step taken by the US was in itself quite objectionable but what made it worse was its timing. The External Affairs

Minister P.V. Narasimha Rao had returned only a week earlier after having very meaningful dialogue with Pak leaders with the hope that new relationship could emerge between the two countries. However the result was resumption of arms race between the two countries. The equipment of Pak army with the F 16 war fighters was a matter of serious concern to India which compelled New Delhi to purchase from Moscow two squadron of MIG-23 fighters which were not a match to F 16 but for the time being we had some deterrent in our hands. The quest for more and better arms went on incessantly with the result that within next four years India acquired Mirag-2000 from France and a couple of years later MIG-29 air defence fighters from the Soviet Union to help counter the F 16s.[14]

US ambassador to India Harry G. Barnes said in New Delhi on 27 February 1982 that in the days of Dulles when arms were being supplied to Pakistan, assurance was given by President Eisenhover himself that the American weapons would not be used against India. But no such guarantee was ever given since then for the obvious reason that no such assurance could be extracted from Pakistan. The US administration did admit their helplessness when on 15 May 1984, Vice-President George Bush reportedly said that there could be no guarantee against the use of US arms to Pakistan against India.[15]

During his visit to the US in October 1985, Rajiv Gandhi conveyed to President Reagan, India's concern over the continued supply of arms to Pakistan but it had no effect on the latter who suggested that the best solution would be for India to improve its relations with Pakistan. He also told Rajiv that with American arms aid Pakistan might abandon its nuclear option. This time Reagan did not stress on his earlier contention that the liberal supply of arms to Pakistan was a part of its proxy offensive against the Soviet controlled Afghan government. However, the US continued to supply various types of sophisticated arms to Pakistan including the AWACS on the plea that it was to defend the western border of Pakistan from repeated incursions of Soviet controlled Afghan regime.[16]

Early in 1987 when the US was going to discuss the second instalment of arms supplies to Pakistan, including AWACS, India felt severely upset. All told, it was going to be a deal worth $4.2 billion. In justification, the old argument was repeated namely the frequent violation of Pakistan's border by Soviet and Afghan aircrafts. Americans forgot the fact that AWACS were ineffective in the mountainous region of Afghanistan, they could be of great value in monitoring Indian air space as well as a significant portion of the Soviet air space in the Tashkent area.[17]

In June 1988 India again approached the US with the suggestion that in the wake of signing of the Geneva accord on Afghanistan, the Soviet forces were bound to leave Afghanistan. In view of this development there was no need to continue to supply arms to Pakistan. Washington viewed the issue from a different angle. Reagan administration further extended aid worth $240 million on the plea that it had already been sanctioned by the Congress for the year 1989.[18] As part of the deal the US supplied 60 F 16 air crafts to Pakistan to which India had already objected. When the Defence Minister, K.C. Pant raised this issue during his visit in June 1989 he was told that Pakistan needed them to replace its aging aircrafts that were supplied to it a decade back.[19]

By mid-1989, Moscow under Michael Gorbachev, withdrew the Soviet troops from Afghanistan and there were rumblings in the U.S. politics for a change in the whole set up. Following this development Pakistan ceased to be a front line state for the US thereby reducing Washington's attention and importance in the South Asian region. Towards the end of 1990, the US administration invoked the Pressler amendment thereby stopping all economic and military aid to Pakistan after President Bush decided that he would not testify that Pakistan did not possess nuclear bomb. Thus ended for the time being US patronage to Pakistan in matters of arms aid.

In the end a word may be said about what had been the US objective in strengthening Pakistan war machine. Among others one was to make it more amenable to a settlement of its problems with India and Bangladesh. This Pakistan could do more easily with American pressure being available in the form of renewed armed support. Secondly, it was also the assumption in the potent political quarters in the US that liberal arms aid to Pakistan would strengthen its confidence in its ability to face the Indian threat whenever it became imminent. But the more solid reason was that by strengthening the defence capability of Pakistan, the US was safeguarding its interests in West Asia. After the fall of the Shah of Iran, the US had lost a reliable ally who was being supported to build up its strong defence in the Gulf and thereby control the entire region. Now the US sought the cooperation of Pakistan to play that role. Besides, by keeping Pakistan gratified the US would extend its interests in the Indian Ocean.

## II

### Pakistan's Nuclear Policy: US Support

The defeat of Pak army in Bangladesh war in 1971 convinced the Pak leadership that in conventional warfare they could not be a match to India and this inadequacy they could make up only by launching a nuclear programme. Bhutto went to the extent of saying that they would eat grass but make a bomb. This he hoped to do only with the help of nuclear powers of which the US seemed to be well disposed. The US took strong exception to India's nuclear experiment in May 1974 and it was believed in Pakistan that the US would not object if Islamabad also decided to go in for such an experiment.

After India's experiment Pakistan started in a clandestine way weapon-oriented programme in which the US connived for reasons best known to it. In 1984, a Pakistani citizen was detected in Houston (Texas) while trying to smuggle electric switches that could be used to trigger nuclear bombs. Another incident occurred on 10 July 1987 when a Pakistani born Canadian citizen was arrested in Philadelphia on charge of trying to steal alloy that could be used in the enrichment of weapon-grade uranium. Such activities could be penalised under the US law passed in 1985. It prohibited the US aid to a country which adopted such clandestine activities to illegally acquire American material and technology for making nuclear arms. The US enjoyed leverage on Pakistan and as such it could dissuade the latter from pursuing such a risky course. India repeatedly asked the US to exercise its influence on Pakistan not to misread India's intentions in launching on a programme of nuclear development for peaceful purposes but to find out how far the two countries could cooperate to achieve a common end. Atal Behari Vajpayee, during his visit to the US in 1979 told the American leaders that Pakistan's pursuit of nuclear weapon capability would lead to nuclear weapon race in the region which would be detrimental to the interests of the entire subcontinent.[20]

Carter administration agreed to some extent with the view expressed by Vajpayee and also urged that India should cooperate with US and other countries to prevent proliferation of nuclear weapons. By implication it meant that Indian example might have provoked Pakistan to set out on acquiring nuclear capability and thereby causing tension in the subcontinent. However, as an immediate step the US administration decided to cut off all economic aid that was earlier earmarked for Pakistan except the food aid which was quite small worth $ 40 million. In the same breath, the US administration was also reported to have suggested to India to the effect that the two countries should enter into a treaty to ban the acquisition of nuclear weapons. In the context of the security scenario of the day such a proposal seemed to be unrealistic.

The US policy underwent a change during the Afghan crisis in which Pakistan became a front line state against the Soviet Union. While continuing a dialogue with Islamabad on nuclear non-proliferation issue, Washington did not make the US military aid to Pakistan contingent upon the latter's assurance to roll back its nuclear weapon programme.[21] President Reagan's attitude was a bit enigmatic. On one hand he was pleading with Pakistan to evolve a formula with India to prevent nuclear proliferation in the subcontinent; on the other, he continued certifying Pakistan's non-possession of nuclear weapons as thereby he could prevail upon the Congress to continue the US aid.

Under the Foreign Assistance Act 1961 the President was empowered to waive the restrictions imposed by the Congress on countries involved in nuclear weapon programme. But the President had to submit a report at the time the waiver authority was exercised to the appropriate committee on foreign affairs stating that the country concerned had not acquired the uranium enrichment capability to the weapon level. While considering the waiver, Senator John Glenn suspected that the Reagan administration had withheld the information about the weapon-making preparation Pakistan was making.[22]

In accordance with the Presidential recommendation the Congress granted a waiver in 1981 to let Pakistan get the most-sophisticated aircrafts F 16 and economic assistance worth $ 3.2 billion during 1981-87. Another instance was witnessed when in August 1987 the US Congress suspended aid to Pakistan for six weeks because of its concern over Islamabad's attempt to smuggle out nuclear weapon oriented material and its refusal to allow the inspection of its Kahuta nuclear plant. But in December 1987 it was restored on the Presidential recommendation with a six-year waiver of Symington amendment facilitating at $ 4.02 billion aid package to Pakistan.[23]

As regards the US suggestion to India to come to an agreement with Pakistan, it was based on some wrong premises. India had repeatedly affirmed that it had no nuclear weapon programme and it was certified by several eminent scientists including Americans. What India wanted was that if Pakistan also declared its commitment to non-nuclear programme and the US assisted it in this process, there would arise no need for any regional agreement. India believed that since Pakistan was bent upon acquiring nuclear weapon capability, the best course leading to peace would be to prevent such a situation in which nuclear proliferation became a reality.

India repeatedly urged the US administration to realise how far their liberal aid for arms development had encouraged Pakistan to think in terms of having their own nuclear capability against India. The US aid helped them to divert a part of their resources to developing nuclear programme. This could be prevented only if the waiver of the Symington amendment was scrapped. This alone would prevent Pakistan from going ahead with its nuclear programme. All this pleading did not yield any result.

However, there were reliable intelligence reports and experts' opinion that Pakistan was on the road of developing nuclear capabilities. A State Department officer submitted before a House of Representative panel in October 1987 that Pakistan might have used its facilities for enriching uranium at a higher level than what was required for peaceful uses.[24] President Reagan himself while issuing certificate in 1986 admitted that by certifying that Pakistan did not possess the bomb, he did not mean to suggest that Pakistan was not attempting to develop a nuclear explosive device or that it had not developed the various relevant capabilities.[25] Despite these declarations, the US continued to help Pakistan with nuclear arsenals.

It was said to be for three reasons; one, that Pakistan had started building nuclear capability as a reaction to India's nuclear programme in this direction, two, any attempt to force Pakistan to conform to US expectations might drive Islamabad towards a full-blown weapon programme.[26] Whatever Pakistan was getting was on a very restricted scale and subject to several constraints but any more constraints Pakistan may not accept. Finally, if the US, in accordance with the Indian suggestion, completely blocked the Pakistani way towards having access to American nuclear expertise, it may irrevocably drive Pakistan to the Chinese camp with consequences too dangerous to think of.

When it appeared that Pakistan was in the process of moving out of the US influence on the nuclear question, Reagan administration and Congress opted to put pressure on India to accept the NPT because Pakistan continued to use the refusal of India to sign the NPT to ward off all US proposals to agree to inspection of its nuclear sites.[27] Accordingly the US Senate adopted a legislation in December 1987 linking India and Pakistan on the nuclear issue. The Senate panel held that Pakistan could not be singled out for enriching nuclear weapon grade material when India too was stockpiling nuclear material.[28]

India took strong exception to this presumption as it equated India's plutonium improving facilities with the clandestinely built uranium enrichment plan in Pakistan. Indian power plants were built under the specific conditions laid down by the international authorities. As regards Pakistani efforts to launch the uranium enrichment process at Kahuta plant, even the US authorities knew that it was being done solely for the weapon manufacturing purposes.[29]

In brief, the legislative measures taken by the US administration meant three things: *(i)* it was a negative signal on the part of US administration to discriminate against India to roll back Pakistan's nuclear weapon making programme, *(ii)* it would have negative influence on Indo-US relation which so many people in both countries had carefully nurtured in recent years; *(iii)* it would generate additional domestic pressure on the government to exercise nuclear option on grounds of national security and also of reasserting our independence–an issue on which Indians were very sensitive.[30]

## REFERENCES

1. *New York Times*, 14 March 1973 cited in P. Sahedevan, p. 590.
2. P. Sahadevan op. cit, p. 594.
3. External Affairs Minister statement, see *Hindustan Times*, 4 May 1973.
4. *Asian Recorder*, 9-15 April 1975, pp. 12533-34
5. *International Herald Tribune*, 16 March 1973 cited in P. Sahadevan, p. 592
6. *Economic Times*, 13 September 1973.
7. *Indian Express*, 5 October 1973

8. *Times of India*, 16 March 1973
9. P. Sahdevan op. cit. P. 594 cites *Asian Recorder*, 21027 May 1975 and the *Statesman*, 27 February 1975
10. *Times of India*, 9 February 1975
11. Dinesh Kumar—*Defence in Indo-US Relations*, p. 29
12. Ibid., p. 23
13. Ibid., p. 32
14. Ibid.
15. *Asian Recorder*, 29 July – 4 August 1984, p. 17865
16. See POT October 1986, Secretary of Defence Casper Weinberger's press conference at Islamabad on 16 October 1986 cited in P. Sahdevan, p. 603
17. Ibid
18 *Indian Express*, 20 March 1989
19 Ibid, 1 July 1989
20 *Hindu*, 7 June 1979
21 P. Sahdevan op. cit., p. 583
22 *Patriot*, 17 May 1987
23 *Hindustan Times*, 31 October 1987
24 *Indian Express*, 19 September 1985
25 P. Sahdevan op. cit., p. 587
26 *Times of India*, 18 December 1988
27 *Amrit Bazar Patrika*, 24 October 1987
28 P. Sahdevan, p. 588
29 *Patriot*, 13 December 1987
30 See *Statesman*, 10 June 1991 for statement by Defence Minister, K.C. Pant

# 9

# Defence Cooperation

In-matters of defence cooperation with India, the US contribution has been very marginal. It was during the Chinese aggression in October 1962 that the US supplied some arms to India but embargo was placed during the Indo-Pak war in 1965. There were no worthwhile defence relations between the two countries for about 8 years between 1965 and 1973 when at the latter date India purchased $ 91 million worth of communication equipment to complete an air radar system installed in the Himalayas. Then came the 1971 war for Bangladesh liberation which began on 3 December 1971. A day before, Washington announced suspension of military sales to India including a $ 70 million air defence communication equipment. On 6 December the US froze all defence deals with India which included $ 87.6 million worth of weaponry which was in pipeline.[1]

After the emergence of Bangladesh as an independent state Pakistan got bifurcated. This event emboldened the US to increase its arms supply to Pakistan on a large scale so much so that during 1976-80 the US arms constituted one fifth of the total of $ 1.8 billion worth weaponry that reached there from different sources. The US share of arms supply to India during this period remained only $ 500 million out of a total of the $ 2.8 billion of arms obtained from several friendly countries the chief being the USSR whose quota was worth $ 2.3 billion.[2]

Urged by strategic considerations, the US government at times felt inclined to have some arms deals with India as such a move would stop India from criticising the US for being the main supplier of arms to Pakistan; it would also go a long way in fostering good relations between the two countries and finally it would reduce India's undue dependence on the Soviet Union for arms supply. India was also eager to diversify its sources of arms supply to different countries. But the terms and conditions proposed by the US were too unreasonable to be acceptable to India.[3]

When in October 1974 Kissinger visited India, he was asked about US arms embargo on the region, but he remained non-committal. On being pressed by Pakistan, the US government lifted the ban on 24 February 1975 resuming weapon supplies to Pakistan though the value involved was merely $ 100 million. On India, the US turned harsh cancelling in January 1976 resumption of aid worth $ 75 million after Washington accused New Delhi of criticising America for attempting to destabilise India.

Till mid 1970s the US was very niggardly in cooperating with India in defence matters. It also tried to see that India did not get weaponry from other sources also. In 1977, the US disapproved sale to India of the Swedes Deep Penetration Strike Aircrafts (DPSA) powered by the American General Electric Company engines. American officials in the Defence establishment said that it was in conformity with its policy of denying sophisticated weaponry to the subcontinent. India eventually settled for the second choice which was the Jagaur strike aircraft manufactured by the British Aerospace.[4]

For the next few years Indo-US relations remained indifferent. Some improvement was witnessed during the Janata regime when Morarji could set up a rapport with President Carter. But in matters of defence cooperation there was not much substantial change which was clear from the fact that between 1976 and 1980 India purchased arms worth 50 million from the US. The deal was small but what was significant from Indian point of view was the US administration's attitude towards Pakistan.

During the period of President Ford, Pakistan was allowed to have A-7 fighter on the old assumption to help Pakistan to keep away from the Chinese influence. But Carter did not give much credence to this view and he disapproved the deal. Another US step taken vis-a-vis Pakistan was appreciated by India. In early 1979 the CIA informed the administration that Pakistan was in the midst of launching a nuclear programme. On receipt of this information, Carter invoked the Symngton amendment which authorised the government to suspend the aid that was being given to Pakistan.

During the Carter days some improvement was made in Indo-US relations. During his visit in January 1978 he was very liberal in paying compliments to the new government under Morarji's stewardship. But in matters of defence cooperation he strictly followed the policy lines laid down by his predecessors. He was reported to have said to his Secretary: 'I told him (Desai) I would authorise the transfer of fuel (for Tarapur nuclear plant) but ... it did not seem to make any impression on him... When we get back, I think we shall write to him another letter, just cold and blunt.[5] Morarji deliberately ignored the gaffe saying that 'remarks not intended to be heard were not heard'.

With the Soviet intervention in Afghanistan on 29 December 1979 Pakistan became a 'front line state' to receive US arms on priority basis. The US administration lifted the Symngton amendment on Pakistan on the plea that Soviet threat over rode other considerations. Initially the offer of $ 400 million offered by the US was disdainfully called as 'peanuts' by Zia-ul Haq. The offer was followed by a high power visit by Carter's security adviser Brzezinski and Defence Secretary Warren Christopher to Pakistan. In accordance with their recommendations more grants were sanctioned. India protested against such a move as the American arms aid would pose a threat to India's security.

President Carter sent Clark Clifford, his special envoy to India to explain the American viewpoint.

In 1980, an Indian military procurement team was sent to America to examine the possibility of purchasing $ 300 million worth arms package comprising some 200 long range 155 mm. guns, 60 Tow launchers and about 4000 anti-tank missiles. The talks were suspended because the US administration did not allow India to make items under licence or to produce the ammunition locally with their technical collaboration after the initial purchase of the war material. India did not accept these conditions. It also opposed the condition that the US had the right to unilaterally cancel the deal without refund of the initial payment.[6]

In mid-eighties, the American view remained dubious. To make a new move, the US, Assistant Secretary of State, Richard Murphy visited India in October 1984 and told the Indian officers that the moment the Afghanistan crisis was over, arms supply to Pakistan would completely be stopped. Meanwhile efforts were made to see that the sophisticated arms that were in the process of being supplied were immediately stopped.

The issue was again raised during Rajiv Gandhi's visit in 1985. The same old argument was put forth namely that the US was arming Pakistan to make that country feel secure, so that it might abandon its nuclear option. The argument was a corollary to the earlier one namely that the US arms sale to Pakistan was linked to the Soviet presence in Afghanistan. Whether Rajiv Gandhi was satisfied with this sort of argument, has been a matter of different interpretations. But the Americans followed their own line of action in supplying various types of weapons on the ground that they had to make Pakistan secure from the Soviet threat.

In September 1985, some Indian scientists went to the US to seek the possibility of procuring the engine for the LCA. They were shown round various establishments to make their choice out of the various products placed before them. The following February a senior officer in the defence technology security establishment Talbot Lindstrom reached New Delhi to assess the areas in which the US could help to strengthen its efficiency in production. India was given 11 of these engines which were to be used in the initial prototype of the LCA. The LCAs were to be fitted with the indigenously developed Kaveri engine.[7]

On 28 February 1985, Kenneth Burns, Deputy Assistant Secretary of Defence visited India to negotiate about duel use equipments which India had asked for. He was followed by Fred Ikle Under Secretary of Defence who before leaving for India admitted on 3 May 1985 that the US long term strategic interests could be secured by providing India with enough advanced weapon technology to turn it into a military power, strong enough to play a major role in global stability late in the century.[8] The American officials now started feeling that it was in the US interest to make India less dependent on the Soviet arms for its security. In their opinion India armed with non-conventional arms would serve their security interests in this region. Among the countries of the democratic West, the US was the only country which could provide India with arms enough to meet its requirements. Thus it was the Soviet factor that largely goaded the US to reorient its policy of arms supply to South Asia in which India would be a major recipient.

The public reactions in America towards the change in their government's policy were quite critical on the ground that India was squandering money on increasing its armed strength ignoring the problems of peoples' hunger disease and illiteracy. But the government view was a little realistic in holding that India's conventional military preparedness was not very advanced to cause concern elsewhere. Besides, the US administration was more liberal in extending economic aid to enable India to solve its problems of poverty and ignorance. Despite the controversy that centered round the US policy in extending arms aid to India, a memorandum of understanding was signed in May 1985 by the two governments to provide India to acquire defence related technology. But when the US officials laid down a precondition of having the right to on site inspection of the nuclear establishment to ensure that there was no diversion of technology to communist countries, particularly the Soviet Union, the Indian side demurred over this clause. The agreement was reached when India agreed to undertake investigation if it suspected any leakage. To appease American sentiments India agreed to associate the US scientists in an enquiry when it would be conducted.

As an additional step towards developing military ties with India the US proposed in 1985 for further interactions between military and defence personnel of the two countries. Under this system Indian army officials would visit the American defence institutes and their American counterparts would come to India. Moreover, Indian officials would make themselves familiar with the use of the sophisticated American weapons that would be manufactured in India under the new agreements. On the production side a group of defence scientists would be associated with the institutions concerned. To start with, this programme would be initiated on a low key basis subject to further expansion if the experience turned out to be beneficial to both the sides.

Another change in American attitude was witnessed when on realising that India was genuninely interested in diversifying its armed acquisition and development programme, it sold in one year 1985 more than $ 12 billion worth of duel-use technology to India. The US Defence department processed more than 3000 Indian cases in 1985 and 92 per cent of them were approved.[10]

In October 1986, the then Secretary of Defence, Weinberger visited India. He assured that the US would continue to help India in various ways including the co-production of various items if cooperation was forthcoming from our side. About two years later, in April 1988 similar sentiments were expressed by his successor, Frank Carlucco. He confirmed American administration's desire to be a partner in India's quest for self-reliance.[11]

The US agreed to supply high-altitude AWACS reconnaissance aircrafts to Pakistan on the ground that they were needed during Afghan conflict. The External Affairs Minister N.D. Tiwari during his visit to Afghanistan in May 1987 found the Afghan government equally critical of the US for destabilising the region with these aircrafts which would be a threat to both the countries. Tiwari cancelled his visit to the USA in protest against the lease of the AWACS to Pakistan which were definitely meant to have a substantial offensive effect against India.[12] Pakistan refuted the allegation that it wanted AWACS in the context of Afghan crisis, but in response to the Indian acquisition of IL-76 surveillance planes from the USSR.[13]

Three important top ranking officials visited India in 1988 – the US Assistant Defence Secretary Richard Armitage; Assistant Secretary of State for South Asia, Richard Murphy and General Vunno, the US Army Chief and met K.C. Pant, Defence Minister and other senior officials in the Defence Ministry. It was made clear to them that India had accepted the US defence technology as it was in tune with its policy of diversifying the sources of its defence purchases. Secondly, despite the assurance of advanced defence related technologies, India would not sign any kind of defence pact with the US as it was liable to be wrongly interpreted in different political quarters.

In 1988, India had to intervene in the crisis in Maldives which the US had approved. This was apparent from the fact that a US navy ship helped the Indian navy in pursuing mercenaries and their hostages. They did not go further and left the matter for the Indian government to settle as it was an issue falling within the sphere of Indian influence. The US did not object to India sending its forces to Sri Lanka as it was a matter mutually decided by the governments of India and Sri Lanka. This showed how the US had started viewing the issues in India's neighbourhood in correct perspective.[14]

Controversy again arose when on 21 May 1989, India successfully test fired Agni, its first Intermediate Range

Ballistic Missile. The U.S administration was pressed to deny India high technological assistance unless it signed the NPT and agreed to place its nuclear facilities to international inspection. Four Congressmen in a memorandum to the President listed three reasons why the US should curb India's missile programme: one, Agni demonstrated India's military threat to Pakistan which would lead to arms race in South Asia; two, Agni testified India's capacity to deliver nuclear war heads; three; India's missile test was in direct contradiction to the efforts of the US and USSR to lessen global tension by reducing ballistic missiles.[15]

In response to the Congressional pressure, Bush administration reacted sharply declaring it as 'a high destabilising development' in the South Asian region. But the administration did not go beyond that; it stuck to its decision to hold a meeting of Indian and American experts to discuss the sale of US technology to India's space programme.[16]

Indian contention was that its missile programme was indigenous and had nothing to do with nuclear weapon making provision. The CIA countered this view and communicated to the government that Indian technology was a product of American and West German transferred technology. On the basis of CIA reports, the supply of space testing equipment approved by the US Commerce Department was held up. The Administration did not go beyond that despite public pressure from certain quarters. The President refused to put a blanket prohibition on technology sale to India on the ground that trade and technology transfer with India remained a stabilising factor towards better bilateral relationship between the two countries.[17]

In brief, whatever items of weaponry India tried to get from the US, Washington's response was delayed and riddled with conditions. It was obviously because of the dissensions among the pro and anti-India lobbies in the US Congress. As an instance, it may be cited that India's request for sale of technology from the American establishment for the development of Akash and Trishul defence missiles was stalled by certain officials in the Defence Department whose aim was to punish India for its arms relationship with Moscow. India on its part, refused to accept an American offer made on 9 March 1989 for a training aircraft along with the complete production facilities on the ground that it would create dependence of India on private defence organisations.

The Defence Minister K.C. Pant's visit to Washington in June 1989, the first after 25 years, gave an opportunity to both sides to discuss common issues of defence cooperation. Instead of making new demands, Pant was anxious to tell his American hosts that the supply of the old items be expedited. He referred to the programme of LCA which had not yet made any headway. He specially asked to examine the possibility of cooperation in respect of certain arms for under water warfare cooperation. With this end in view he sought US submarine technology system which would enable India to indigenously manufacture a submarine fleet.[18] To boost further defence cooperation, the American side also suggested the idea of conducting a joint naval exercise in the Indian Ocean. Pant was a little reluctant to accept the offer as it might be given a political colour and India may be regarded as having come to some military alliance with the USA. As an alternative he agreed on a greater service-to-service exchange between India and the US.[19]

During the Gulf war the US was building its forces in Saudi Arabia. V.P. Singh, then Prime Minister allowed refuelling on Indian soil of US military aircrafts on supplying runs from the Philippines to Persian Gulf. This helped the US airforce to operate their military transport aircrafts with full load capacity. This decision was criticised by a big section of public opinion compelling the successor government of Chandra Shekhar to cancel the permission for refuelling.

In the second half of 1991, Indo-US relations received a further impetus when the C-m-C of the US Pacific Army Lt. General Clark KickLeighter mooted the proposal which envisaged extended cooperation and partnership between the two countries. Consequently an advisory Executive Steering

Group (ESG) was set up in January 1992 followed by one each for the navy and air force in March 1992 and April 1993 respectively. Under the auspices of these bodies the first ever military to military level exercise began on a regular scale.

## REFERENCES

1. Dinesh Kumar—Defence in Indo-US Relations, p. 20.
2. Palmer, *The United States and India*, p. 190, cited, P. Sahdeva, p. 615
3. *Times of India*, 27 July 1982
4. Dinesh Kumar op. cit., p. 29
5. Ibid, p. 30
6. Ibid., p. 31
7. Ibid., p. 39
8. P. Sahdevan op. cit., p. 616
9. *Telegraph (Calcutta)*, 23 May 1985
10. For U.S. Defence Secretary Casper Weinberger's report to the Congress, see *Times of India* 8 July 1987.
11. Dinesh Kumar, op. cit. p. 40
12. *Annual Report* 1987, Defence Ministry, Government of India, p. 2.
13. J.N. Parimoo in *Times of India*, 19 February 1988
14. Dinesh Kumar, op. cit., p. 40
15. P. Sahdevan op. cit. P. 613
16. For the Statement of White House spokesman, see *Amrit Bazar Patrika*, 21 May 1989 cited in P. Sahdevan, p. 14
17. *Times of India*, 7 July 1989
18. P. Sahdevan, p. 620
19. *Hindu*, 11 July 1989

# 10

# The Nuclear Factor

The proliferation issue remained a potent factor causing differences between the relations of the two countries. It became all the more serious ever since India experimented with its nuclear device in May 1974 and, as a counter move the US insisted that India sign the NPT. Considering it as a discriminatory document India refused to do that, though it repeatedly reaffirmed that it remained opposed to nuclear proliferation and that it was committed to use nuclear technology only for peaceful purposes. But this assurance did not carry much conviction with the American policy makers. They, on the other hand, as a punitive step started delaying supply of enriched uranium to India's Tarapur atomic plant.

Even in the friendly days of Carter regime, the US did not relent to make any effort to meet India's view point. In his times, two legislative measures were passed: Glenn – Symington amendment in 1977 and Nuclear Non-proliferation Act in 1978. Both, in essence, envisaged that the US would cut off economic assistance to any country which would not accept internationally approved safeguards for its nuclear facilities or that it pursued nuclear programme aimed at developing nuclear weapons' capabilities.[1] The spillover effects of these legislative measures had their impact on Indo-US relations which both sides regretted.

When much pressure was brought to bear on the government, Morarji Desai reiterated that India would neither accept international inspection nor sign the NPT 'as long as the nuclear weapon powers did not put an end to its discriminatory character'. He sought the nuclear weapon powers to fulfill three conditions in this respect. (i) all of them stop nuclear tests, (ii) they stop adding to their nuclear stockpile and decide to progressively dismantle their nuclear weapons and (iii) they themselves accept full scope safeguards.[2] He held the nuclear powers responsible for creating more nuclear proliferation as they refused to reduce their nuclear arsenal and it is from them that the nuclear threat would emanate. This was the view held by the successive governments also. For instance Rajiv Gandhi during his US visit in June 1985 described the NPT as a 'blatantly unfair' document which in his view should not be in existence.

In the mid-eighties, there was some ominous change in the US attitude which sought to expect both India and Pakistan to toe the American line on matters of nuclear proliferation. The Senate passed a resolution in December 1987 urging both India and Pakistan to sign the NPT, accept international safeguards and accept inspection of each other's nuclear facilities.[3] The idea behind this move was that Pakistan was refusing to sign the NPT on the plea that India was also not prepared to do that. Now Pakistan was bracketed with India with the motive that Pakistan's agreement to sign the NPT would enable the USA to exert pressure on India.

India objected to being told that Pakistan's inability to sign the NPT was borne out of India's refusal to adhere to the treaty. It was urged that the motives of the two governments in following their nuclear policies were quite different and the issue be viewed objectively. But the US administration struck to its own decision. In an amendment adopted on 7 December 1987, the Senate clearly laid down that the US administration would be free to block, not only the flow of high technology items to India but also vote against the grant of World Bank by portraying its nuclear development programme as weapon oriented.[4] Pakistan was also not spared; the aid worth $ 4.2 billion which was earlier sanctioned was suspended.

Realising that the amendment amounted to double punishment to India, stoppage of supply of high technology and suspension of the aid, the government took up the issue with the US administration. There was much out cry in the country as the American move was a pressure to influence the fundamentals of our foreign policy. India only wanted that in any policy formulation India should not be linked with Pakistan. The reasons why we did not subscribe to the terms of NPT were those which Pakistan should have also endorsed. But to accept India's policy as a condition for Pakistan's adherence to the treaty was at once illogical and irrelevant.[5]

India's persistent efforts succeeded in influencing the Reagan administration to exert pressure on the Senate to reverse the controversial amendment. Consequently, the Senate on 12 December 1987, adopted a reconciliatory measure whereby the high technology transfer and defence equipment's sales to India were to be continued. But India's grievance that it should not be linked with Pakistan on the non-proliferation issue remained unattended. It was obviously because the Senate was favourably disposed to the continuation of military and economic aid worth $ 4.2 billion to Pakistan despite its weapon oriented nuclear programme.[6]

## Nuclear Fuel Issue

The US continued to supply the enriched uranium to the atomic power plant at Tarapur (TAPS) under the agreement signed between the two countries in 1963. The US was fairly regular in supplying this commodity to the TAPS which was built with the US assistance. But with the explosion of the nuclear device in 1974, differences started to grow between the two countries. The US administration was very susceptible to the public opinion in the country which began to doubt the motives of the Indian government to pursue nuclear research for peaceful uses only. The US could have unilaterally abrogated the 1963 agreement but it would have been too drastic a step as a protest against India's going nuclear.

The US administration realised well that the safeguards embodied in the 1963 agreement were quite effective in preventing the plutonium products from being diverted to military use. Still the State Department further sought India's commitment to abide by the treaty provisions. India gave a prompt pledge to follow strictly all the safeguards of the agreement. Further, a team of American atomic scientists visited Tarapur in November 1975 to inspect the working of the plant and report deviation, if any, they had observed in its working. The report was quite positive and the US Atomic Energy Commission was convinced of India's bonafides.[7] But for political reasons some Congressmen continued to insist that the supply of nuclear fuel to India be linked with the acceptance of the NPT and full scope nuclear safeguards.

However, the trouble again cropped up when India on 5 November 1975 approached the US Nuclear Regulating Commission (NRC) to sanction the supply of an additional shipment of fuel for Tarapur. The US administration supported India's demand on the ground that any failure on their part would cause 'severe economic and social damage' to India, and it would be a severe set back to Washington's efforts to improve its relations with New Delhi. The supporters strongly reaffirmed that their supply performance with respect to India would strongly influence American reputation for reliability with other nations. There was no justification in delaying or denying the supply when India had not violated any understanding given to the US by the 1963 agreement and any delay in the export of nuclear fuel would result in irreparable damage to the foreign relations of the US.[8]

Despite such cogent arguments stated in favour of India, some environmentalists and scientists urged the NRC to with hold the supply on the ground that such a step would increase the danger of world wide nuclear proliferation and help India divert its nuclear capacity into military weaponry. They also pointed out that despite US appeals India had not signed the NPT nor placed the Tarapur facilities under the 'safeguard inspection' of the International Atomic Energy Agency (IAER).

Indian government gave their arguments in support of what they wanted from the US. India reminded that the provisions of 1963 agreement were so specific that India or, for that matter, any other non-nuclear power receiving nuclear fuel from the US could not use the fuel for any other purpose not stated in the agreement. Secondly, the role of the IAEA in inspecting nuclear facilities was getting so comprehensive that on the slightest doubt they could declare that India was likely to divert the nuclear material to weapon-making. This was totally unwarranted by the ethics of scientific dealings. Finally, a team of scientists, from the NRC and members of the various agencies concerned had inspected the facilities in India in November 1975.[9] The report was a categorical assertion of India's bonafides in its nuclear dealings with the US.

The NRC gave clearance to fuel shipments. The agreement provided that the shipment of the fuel would continue up to 1976, the year when the 1963 agreement would end so that Tarapur's power production would neither be curtailed nor slowed down, at least till the end of 1976. The NRC could not say anything about what would be the position after 1976. It confined its judgement to the period stated in the 1963 agreement.

President Carter's assumption of office in 1976 gave a new turn to this issue. He was positively in favour of improving relations with India. In January 1978, he was in India and as a result of his assessment of the worth of Indian leadership he felt convinced that they were trustworthy and would stand by what they said. In June 1977 Carter administration approached the NRC to sanction the shifting to India of 12.261 kg. of uranium meant for use for the next six months. In support of the case he said, the US had binding contract with India as a fuel supplier; India had complied with the US safeguards in the working of the

Tarapur plant; India's new Janata leadership was far more to be trusted under Morarji Desai than what it may have been under Mrs. Gandhi, and the US policy had not denied fuel supplies to other countries, which had not placed all their nuclear facilities under the overall IAEA safeguards.[10]

The NRC accepted the arguments put forth by the Carter administration holding that withholding action on the present licence would be inconsistent not only with the nation's general policy of being a reliable supplier of nuclear fuel but also with the encouraging response thus far received from India on this issue. Finally, the supply of reactor fuel to India would assist the US in its forthcoming negotiations with India. At the same time keeping in view the objections from a section of scientists, the NRC warned that the US would terminate the supply of fuel to Tarapur if India decided to repeat its 1974 nuclear experiment even for peaceful purposes, even with entirely indigenously provided material and utilising technology not directly received from the USA.

In August 1977, Carter sent a ranking official, Joseph Nye to discuss more issues relevant to nuclear policies. He tried to explain why the US insisted on the enforcement of safeguards and on site inspection of the nuclear facilities of those which had received nuclear aid from the US. This was not specifically directed against India.

During his visit to India in January 1978, Carter informed Desai that the US Congress was intending to enact a legislation in August 1978 which would require any country buying nuclear fuel from the US to accept on site inspection of power plants using the fuel. When he found the intensity of India's nuclear nationalism, he announced in his address to the members of Parliament that he would send another shipment of nuclear fuel of 7.6 tons for Tarapur.[11] But in view of the new legislation passed by the Congress the NRC refused to sanction its despatch on the ground of India's non-acceptance of full scope safeguards. There was much outcry in India as it amounted to a breach of 1963 agreement.

Carter overruled the NRC's decision and signed the document on 27 April 1978 approving the licence for the shipment of 7.6 tons of enriched uranium to Tarapur. He justified his decision on the ground that the US nuclear fuel was meant only for Tarapur and not for any explosion and military purpose. In his view, their denial of the export would seriously undermine their efforts to persuade India to accept full scope safeguards and prejudice the achievement of other US non-proliferation goals.[12]

During his visit to the US in June 1978 Desai tried to mobilise the Congressional and American public opinion in India's favour. He urged that India should not be singled out for disfavour by a friendly country like the US through a unilateral modification of its contractual obligation. He reaffirmed India's commitment to act in the spirit of safeguards though it may not sign an agreement to that effect.[13]

In March 1979 the NRC further approved the shipment of 18.5 tons of additional tons of enriched uranium. But the problem arose when the grace period of 18 months provided for in the legislation of 1978 came to an end on 10 March 1980. On 7 May 1980 the State Department announced that the US would not supply any nuclear fuel for TAPS because of Indian government's refusal to abide by full scale nuclear safeguards. Probably influenced by the public pressure, the NRC on 16 May 1980 unanimously voted against granting an export licence for the shipment of uranium to India. There was a pressure from the Congressional quarters also but Carter remained firm and on 19 June 1980 signed the order authorising pending shipment of 38 tons of fuel. The President in his letter to the Congress justified his action on the ground that if the US had broken the existing agreement, India would be relieved of its obligations to refrain from reprocessing the fuel previously supplied by the US.[14]

The President further stated that the refusal of nuclear fuel would cast a long shadow on the overall relationship between the two countries. Moreover, the NRC had adopted a more restrictive interpretation of the grace period; in fact the application fell within the grace period. The administration believed that the Indian government would use nuclear energy for peaceful purposes. Also the administration felt that the Soviet Union would exploit a refusal by the US to supply fuel to India and might well supplant Washington as the source of Tarapur fuel. There was a heated discussion in both the Houses of the Congress on this issue. The House of Representative voted on 18 September 1980 to block the sale of nuclear fuel to India but the Senate by a narrow margin of two votes supported the President's decision. Thus a short-term solution of the issue was achieved.[15]

Regan administration took a tough position in this respect. An Indian delegation headed by Homi Sethna, Chairman of the Atomic Energy Commission visited Washington on 16-17 April 1981 to hold discussions on this issue. It was clearly told that the US would not be able to continue the fuel supply relationship and also that even after India was denied its rights under the bilateral agreement, it would continue to be bound by the Tarapur safeguards not to reuse the spent fuel properties.[16]

In view of this deadlock, the only option left to the two countries was to terminate the 1963 agreement through mutual consent. In this connection India suggested that in the event of the US withdrawing its commitment to supply enriched uranium to TAPs, India would be under no obligation to place TAP under international safeguards. This was not acceptable to the US. This deadlock was solved to some extent during Mrs. Gandhi's visit to Washington in July 1982. It was agreed by both the countries that France would replace the US as supplier of nuclear fuel to TAP and that all other conditions and obligations envisaged in the 1963 agreement remained in effect.[17] This agreement suited both the countries. The US was saved from the embarrassment of acknowledging a breach of contract and at the same time placed Tarapur plant under international safeguards. The US scored another important point. By accepting France as a supplier of uranium fuel, Washington denied the USSR a chance to enter into possible nuclear cooperation with India. Thus the nuclear fuel issue was mutually settled to the satisfaction of both the countries.

## REFERENCES

1. P. Sahedevan op. cit. p. 556
2. His talk to a team of American TV interviews in 1978. See *Statesman*, 5 January 1978.
3. *Amrit Bazar Patrika* 7 August 1987
4. *Hindu*, 5 December 1987
5. For the statements of Indian leaders see *Asian Recorder* 1988, p. 19849
6. P. Sahedavan, p. 560
7. P. Sahedavan, p. 562
8. *Statesman*, 26 March 1976
9. Ibid., 1 July 1977
10. P. Sahedavan, p. 565
11. See *Times of India*, 3 January 1978
12. P. Sahedavan, p. 570
13. *Statesman*, 16 June 1978
14. The text of the message published in *Patriot* 21 June 1978
15. See for details *Indian Express* 20 June 1980 from T.V. Parasuram in Washington
16. Ibid., 11 September 1980
17. *Asian Recorder*, 27 August - 2 September 1982, p. 16761

# 11

# Economic and Scientific Interactions

As a reaction to the 1971 war in Bangladesh the US aid was suspended and this remained in force till 1977. But it did not affect the PL 480 aid a part of which, amounting to $ 85 million was given in 1972. Likewise the American decision did not affect the flow of American assistance through multi-national institutions such as International Development Association in which the US had a decisive say.[1]

In the post-Bangladesh period, India also did not like the idea of approaching the US for economic aid partly because India wanted to reduce its economic dependence on the US for political reasons and partly because with the advent of 'green revolution', India had become almost self-sufficient on the food front. So far India depended mostly on food grains supplied by the US to make up its food deficit. The US also wanted to do away with its traditional aid pattern and adopt a policy in the implementation of which it would have a low profile in bilateral economic assistance. The Mutual Development and Cooperation Act stipulated that the bilateral development aid would be concentrated on the urgent problems of the majority in developing countries—food nutrition, health education and rural development.[2]

Now the main problem between the two countries was how to settle the issue of American blocked rupee accounts mostly arising from the PL 480 agricultural product sales to India. As a result of the prolonged discussions between the two sides, an agreement was signed in New Delhi on 18 February 1974 providing the procedure for the disposal of PL 480 rupees. According to this agreement, India would provide pre-payment to the US of all remaining sums it owed to that country. That amount was expected to be Rs. 15140 million. The US would cash its securities with the Reserve Bank of India which amounted to Rs. 1870 million. The total of the two would come to Rs. 17010 million out of which the US would grant to India Rs. 16640 million representing the substantial portion of the pre-payment of PL 480 commodities loans. This would be a net gain to India which according to the agreement, would gradually accrue within a period of five years.[3]

After the rupee debt agreement, there was little prospect of the US aid resumption to India though the administration was authorized to give to India a debt up to $ 75 million a year. The immediate cause of resentment was India's nuclear test in May 1974. Again talks were initiated in early 1976 but Mrs. Gandhi's statement that the US was carrying out a "Chilean-style" destabilisation campaign in India annoyed the administration so much that they refused to have any talk with her representatives on any issue, much less on economic aid.[4]

With the change of governments in both the countries early in 1977, a new atmosphere came into being in which talks between the two sides could be initiated. Accordingly a high official level talks were held in New Delhi in Mid-1977 on the possible resumption of direct US aid to India. The talks continued for several months and a final agreement was concluded on 26 August 1978. Under the agreement the US was committed to give India $ 58 million in soft loans and $ 2 million in grant. Both were meant to be utilised for rural welfare plans. The loans were repayable in 40 years with a 10-year grace period at very low interest. Subsequently the Congress approved $ 60 million and $ 90 million soft loans to India for the financial year 1978-79.[5]

When in 1979 Carter administration prepared a development aid of $ 135 million to India, it was opposed in the Congressional circles on the ground that India had three good crop years and also had foreign exchange reserves of $ 7 billion. Thus India did not need any more aid from the US. Carter's successor Reagan sought to reduce the level of US aid to India as its foreign policy postures were not in the best interests of the USA. He cited two events in support of his decision; Indian shipment of food for the Soviet Union and its aid to Vietnam in the early eighties. But under political pressure he yielded stating that India was a major power in Asia and that it had a democratic constitutional government at home working successfully.[6] So it could act independently to safeguard its own interests with or without US aid.

In the early eighties, despite some uneasiness caused by the Afghan crisis, the US was reasonably responsive to India's need for economic assistance. In 1980, credits totalling $35 million was extended for financing some development proposals and in 1981, the assistance amounted to $ 110 million besides a PL-480 aid of $ 419 million. According to the statement of Finance Minister Pranab Mukherji in the Lok Sabha on 15 April 1983 India had taken loans aggregating $ 399.6 million from the USA during October 1977—September 1982.[7]

Another development be noted in this context. The US Congress adopted a mandate authorising the US administration to stop foreign assistance to a country which was engaged in a consistent pattern of opposition to foreign policy of the US in the UN and reduce the contribution to the UN and other international agencies to which the US contributed for the sake of developing countries. This was a very invidious move as it would mean that if India wanted to be benefited by the US assistance, it would have to toe the American policy on all international issues. Criticism of American policy would be used as an excuse to deny US assistance to India. Mrs. Gandhi observed that by this policy the US would assume 'a confrontationist attitude towards others.[8] This policy found its practical implementation in August 1987 when the Foreign Affairs Committee of the House of Representatives cut down the development assistance from the proposed amount of $ 60 million to $ 35 million on the tacit understanding that India's foreign policy towards Israel was not to the liking of the US. The resolution urged India to improve its relations with Israel as the growth of contacts between the two countries would benefit both the countries.[9] This condition evoked India's adverse reactions which were conveyed to the US government through diplomatic channels.

In 1988, the USAID assistance was drastically reduced from $ 50 million in the previous year to a mere $24 million for reasons of 'shortage of funds'. But this again was attributed to the US disapproval of India's stand on some international issues in which the US was involved. To express its resentment, the US administration extended liberal aid to countries like Israel, Egypt and Pakistan whose cooperation the US appreciated in the conduct of proxy wars or in implementing other foreign policy priorities.[10]

Again an attempt was made in June 1989 in the form of an amendment in the Congress to this effect that the aid of $ 25 million to be given to India in the fiscal year 1990-91 should be limited to a certification by the President that India made significant progress in reducing human rights abuses in Punjab and ended its economic blockade of Nepal. India was also faulted for not condemning the Soviet Union for its invasion of Afghanistan. With the Congressmen belonging to India lobby opposing it, the amendment was lost by 272 to 203 votes. The small margin victory indicated the trends in the public opinion of the US. This marked the beginning of the end of Indian efforts to seek US aid even for causes of purely economic and scientific development with the result that the US aid ceased to be a substantial factor in economic development of India. What was very objectionable to India was that the issues of economic aid were governed by the foreign policy considerations.[11]

**Bilateral Trade**

The US has been India's principal trade partner in the sense that it has been the main source of India's imports as well as a major market of Indian goods. Prior to 1974, the trade between the two countries was carried on an ad-hoc basis with no prepared plan envisaging an over all view of trade prospects. In that year an Indo-US joint commission was set up to facilitate exchange in the fields of trade and commerce. The Commission at its meeting in Washington on 7 October 1975 agreed to establish a joint business council consisting of businessmen of both the countries which would look into the details to stimulate trade promotions in each country through means like trade missions and trade shows. As a result of the efforts made by the joint commission, India was designated in 1976 as a beneficiary of the Generalised System of Preference (GSP) scheme under which the US permitted duty free imports of 2724 articles from India. This gave India the necessary competitive edge vis-a-vis imports from other sources notably Canada, West Europe and other developed countries of East Asia such as Japan since imports of the same items from there would be taxed.[12]

In the early seventies the US enjoyed a favourable balance in Indo-US trade. As an illustration, during the year 1971-73, the annual Indian exports to the US totalled about $ 400 million, which was about 15 per cent of total exports whereas imports from the US were about $ 500 millions roughly 18 per cent of India's total imports. In 1975, the position was also unfavourable with exports to the US amounting to $ 548 million and imports totalling $ 1287 million causing a trade gap of $ 741.5 million. In 1976, India's exports rose by 29.5 per cent reaching the figure of $ 710.2 million and imports from the US declined by 12 per cent to $ 1134.7 million causing a trade gap of $ 424.5 million. This deficit was said to be due to foodgrain shortage in India which continued till 1976 and till then the American wheat supply was the sole source of sustenance.[13]

In 1977 India scored a favourable balance selling $ 894.2 million worth of goods to US and buying only $ 760.1 million worth American goods thus netting a favourable trade balance of $ 34.1 million. The main reason for this gain was India's stopping to buy American wheat during the year. In 1979, though India's total trade turnover exceeded the $ 2 billion, it had a trade deficit of $ 122 million against a trade surplus of $ 3.8 million during 1978 and $ 34.1 million during 1977. Exports from India recorded a rise of $ 57 million or 5.9 per cent in 1979 as compared to 1978. This was, however, much lower than this increase of $ 218 million or 23 per cent in 1977 which was higher than the increase of $ 168 million or 21.6 per cent in 1978.[14] The year 1979 turned out to be unfavourable to India as though the total trade turnover exceeded the $ 2 billion mark, India had a deficit of $ 122 million.

Though the US continued to enjoy a favourable trade balance, it, for reasons of its own, decided to take some measures in early eighties which threatened to affect India's exports substantially to that country. In 1980, the US administration imposed countervailing duties, ranging from 2.5 per cent to 20 per cent on a number of exports from India on the assumption that this would offset what the Indian government allegedly gave as cash compensatory support and subsidies.

As a result a large number of importers in the US cancelled orders and thus a number of industrial units which relied on US market were threatened with closure. Further, the US issued a notification to GATT excluding India from getting benefit on subsidies. After a prolonged discussion the US lifted the duties on textiles but others continued.[15]

An overview of Indo-US trade relations shows that the two-way trade increased from about Rs. 682 crores in 1971-72 to about Rs. 2304 crores in 1981-82. It amounted to about 11 per cent of India's total exports aid 12 per cent of India's total imports. The year 1983 was a bit lucky as because of the Bombay high crude, this country achieved a large favourable balance of trade totalling nearly $ 400 million with the US in 1983. According to the figures for January-October

1983, India's exports to the US during the period reached a record level of $ 852.2 million whereas imports remained at $ 1530.02 million resulting a balance of trade totalling $ 322 million in favour of India during this period.[16]

Although US remained India's biggest trading partner, the rate of increase in the volume of trade was not fast enough or proportionate to the size of sub-continental economy. One of the reasons for this was that both the countries imposed barriers on their trade relations with each other. A large number of import items were on the banned list in India and the US continued to increase the tariff barriers that impeded the growth of Indian exports to the US.[17]

During the Indo-US trade talks in New Delhi on 13-14 December 1986. India referred to the damage caused to its trade interests in several items because of the repeated use of countervailing duty anti-dumping measures and other such devices. Indian delegation pointed out that many of their restrictions were not in conformity with the GATT code. One industry which was affected most was the textile which was clear from the fact that India's share of the American market for clothing had fallen from 3.25 per cent in 1970 to 2.4 per cent in 1984. The U.S. administration realised the validity of Indian argument and in February 1987 signed an agreement which was meant to boost India's textile exports to the US by 7 per cent per annum for the next 5 years.[18]

In 1985 the quantum of Indian exports was higher in a total volume of $ 4.1 billion but in the next year the balance turned adverse to the extent of $ 900 million in the total two-way trade of $ 4 billion. Again in 1987 this trend was changed in favour of India when Indian exports rose from $ 1951.3 million in January—December 1986 to $ 2138.2 million during the same period in 1987 but the imports from the US were down to $ 1171 million from the previous years' figure of $ 1248.3 million.[19] The significant aspect of India's trade with the US in the late eighties was that in the 1960s and 1970s foodgrains constituted more than half of all US imports to India. In the 1980s technology sales took their place. For instance in 1983, the US high technology rates to India accounted for $ 300 million, it increased to $ 526 million in 1988. The bilateral trade in 1988 was estimated at $ 5.7 billion, a record of 37 per cent increase. The American business community came with their latest technology when they participated in the international engineering trade fair in New Delhi from 19 to 26 February 1989.

A very unpleasant situation arose when in 1989, the Bush administration singled out India, along with Brazil and Japan to accuse them of unfair trade practice against US interests. The idea was to invoke 'Super 301' provision of US trade and competitiveness Act of 1988 which provided that if those countries failed to remove identified barriers during the next 18 months (since May 1989) duties on their exports to the US could be levied by as much as 100 per cent on some items. India was particularly cited for restrictions in trade related investment, such as requirements placed on foreign investors to export a portion of what they produced or to sell locally produced inputs in their manufactures. It was also cited for closing its markets completely to foreign insurance companies.

India objected to this move on the plea that India ran a trade surplus of only $ 670 million with the US, out of a total bilateral trade of $ 5.7 billion whereas Japan had a trade surplus of $ 55.4 billion with the US. In making this allegation, Washington should have taken note of the fact that in the overall trade volume during 1988 which rose by 15 per cent, the US exports expanded by 65 per cent. The US thus acquired the position of being the largest trading partner of India which position had so far been occupied by the USSR.[20]

India's grievance was more serious in so far as while negotiations were going to take place to rectify some minor trade issues, the US decided to take unilateral action under cutting the multilateral process. It was also in violation of the US commitments under the GATT. As regards, US complaint that India had banned the entry of foreign insurance companies it amounted to interfering in our internal matters. No country had the right to suggest that India should keep open its markets for foreign interests. Finally when the US had built and retained certain barriers against access to its own markets, it could not ask others to lift barriers without doing so itself.

President Bush in his rejoinder said that lack of multilateral rules and enforcement had forced the US to use the Super 301 provisions of the trade law to eliminate trade restrictions. He invited India to resume the dialogue instead of getting irritated. Rajiv Gandhi refused to have any discussion on the issue of Super 301 as it would amount to acting on some foreign powers' dictates. India also told the GATT Council in June 1985 that participating countries would find it extremely difficult to negotiate under threat of unilateral retaliations which caused uncertainties for India's trade.[21]

The Indian government was strongly supported in its opposition to the US action by the various national trade organisations in the opinion of which, India would suffer if some united opposition was not put up against this move. Besides, the trade representatives of Japan, Brazil, and some EEC countries also considered the US move as unfair. Under this pressure, the US had to soften its stand. The US trade representatives had made their assessment on identification on 25 May 1989 and the proceedings would have been started on 15 June 1989, when the 3 week period was over. The US administration deferred to take any action but on the other hand conveyed the impression to the Indian officials that the government did not favour the sanction of the 'Super 301' but the action was a result of the constraints of US law. Thus ended an unhappy controversy that created much tension on both sides. Despite the interregnum, trade flow continued to remain unabated. It reached a peak level of $ 5.5 billion in 1988 with a surplus of $ 600 million in India's favour. The surplus was set to cross the one billion dollar mark in 1989.

## Science and Technology

The Indo-US cooperation in the field of science and technology began in early seventies but the main thrust was given only after Mrs. Gandhi's visit to the US in 1982. As a result of talks between Mrs. Gandhi and President Reagan in July 1982, a panel of scientists of the two countries to chalk out a detailed programme was formed in 1983. The panel at its meeting in New Delhi on 31 January 1983 suggested four broad areas of cooperation, agriculture, public health, earth sciences and material research. These were meant to extend maximum benefits to the rural backward community all over the country in so far as they would provide food, fodder, shelter and public health to the needy masses.

In sharing the secrets of higher technology the US had two reservations, one, that it might be put to military use, two it might be shared with countries of the Soviet bloc. But India was not prepared to accept any condition which would compel it to subject its technological achievements to any outside inspection and secrutiny as it would amount to a compromise with our sovereign rights. President Reagan realised the force in this arguments and later agreed to clear the way for a major agreement which was signed on 8 March 1985 on transfer of higher technology to India. Under this deal technological institutions already working on subjects in which American scientists would feel interested to help their Indian counterparts to achieve excellence in the sphere of the subject would get further assistance.[22]

This was indeed a major break through in the scientific relations between the two countries but it had a political slant. Reagan was serious to create atmosphere of good will between the two countries prior to Rajiv Gandhi's visit to the US in June 1985.[23] However, for public consumption it was held out that the American administration's commitment was to build up India's strong scientific and technological base. A month later the sub-commission on science and technology at its meeting held in New Delhi on 8 April 1985, recommended the establishment of an intercontinental telecommunication link to enable India to use US data base and US know how in the use of computers as educational aids and also in the development of improved vaccine to be used in the field of public health.[24]

The interest of the US administration in the defence matters was apparent when in the wake of the visit of US Under Secretary of State for Defence Fred Ikla to India in May 1985, it discussed matters related to the transfer of high technology. For fear of Soviet spying the agreement precluded India's accessibility or transfer of technology in sensitive defence and nuclear fields; it limited the availability of US technology to computer electronics and telecommunications. The Americans claimed that safeguards by which India had to abide, were applicable to all the countries with which the US had signed similar agreements.[25]

The efforts made by the two countries to have close scientific relations clearly suggested that the US was willing to help India on those minor issues which would make a good beginning in the confidence building process. During Rajiv Gandhi's visit, two such minor agreements were signed, one was to develop and produce new and improved vaccines against major communicable diseases and the other a long term research and technology development programme covering activities in agriculture, forestry, family welfare and bio-medical research. Reagan assured US cooperation in reducing pollution of larger river systems. In the wake of Rajiv's visit, the US administration approved the sale of $ 50 million worth of high technology to India. The sales were part of earlier agreement that enabled India to buy $894 million worth of American products in the fiscal year 1985. This was merely $ 400 million more than what was allowed to buy a year earlier.[26]

Again when India asked for the supply of super computers with which it would watch the movements of the monsoons and the approximate time of seasonal rains, the US administration expressed its inability to do so. Two reasons seemed to have prompted the US to take this unpleasant step, the US distrust in the bonafides of India and the possibility of nuclear programme falling in the hands of Soviet spies. The President was under political pressure not to rely on assurances given by the recipient countries not to use the technology for nuclear purposes but he should insist on enforcing the safeguards which were meant for all the countries India being no exception to it.

1987 turned out to be the year in which the two governments signed several agreements. In March 1987, a joint forum was instituted by the two governments to finance joint ventures on subjects of science in which both the governments would be interested. Priority was given to combat AIDs for which the US experts offered to contribute their cooperation. A memorandum of understanding was signed on 9 July 1987 to develop a project aimed at providing inexpensive vaccines for diseases which were common in rural areas. The five year project was estimated to cost $9.6 million of which the US would contribute $ 7.6 million. India's contribution was $ two million.[27]

The Indo-US sub-commission on science at its meeting on 5 November 1987 identified several new areas in the field of environment and ecology and other related sciences, the research in which would lead to contribute to the mitigation of the problems of poverty and disease among the poor sections of the society. About eleven projects in areas of food processing and other related matters were undertaken.

Further impetus was given to the cooperation in science and technology during the second non-state visit of Rajiv Gandhi in 1987. An agreement was signed to work out a programme of collaboration in research in Ocean science and climate research. The agreement envisaged cooperation in research projects designed to enhance productivity in arid zone agriculture and exploration of water resources. The year also witnessed transfer of technology on a liberal scale, the approval going up to 900 high technology components valued at $ 28 billion to India.[28] Nearly one third of US exports to India in the year were of high technology products.

## REFERENCES

1. P. Sahdevan op. cit. p. 630.
2. See *Economic Times*, 13 September 1973 for Henry Kissinger's statement on 11 September 1973
3. P. Sahdevan op. cit. p. 631
4. *International Herald Tribune*, 18 February 1976 cited in P. Sahdevan, p. 634
5. P. Sahdevan, p. 638
6. See *Tribune*, 13 May 1982 for statement by S. Staples, Head of Asian Affairs at the US Agency for International Development
7. See *Indian Express*, 16 April 1983
8. See *Asian Recorder*, 1-7 April 1984, p. 17676 for Mrs. Gandhi's press interview with the Associated News on 22 January 1984.
9. *Asian Recorder*, 8-14 October 1987, p. 19686
10. *Hindustan Times*, 31 January 1988
11. See, P. Sahdevan p. 639
12. See P. Sahdevan, p. 641
13. *Hindustan Times*, 7 March 1977
14. The Statesman, 5 January 1978
15. Ibid., 5 August 1980 and *Indian Express*, 11 September 1980
16. See P. Sahdevan p. 644
17. Ibid
18. *Indian Express*, 14 December 1986
19. *Economic Times*, 28 January 1988
20. *Hindu*, 27 May 1989
21. P. Sahdevan, p. 650
22. P. Sahdevan op. cit., p. 622

23. *Asian Recorder*, 23-29 April 1985 p. 18281

24. *Telegraph*, 11 April 1985

25. US Ambassador Harry Barn's statement, see P. Sahdevan, p. 624

26. *International Herald Tribune*, 16 October 1985

27. *Asian Recorder*, 27 August – 2 September 1987, p. 19616

28. *Economic Times*, 23 January 1987

# 12
# The Miscellany

## Indian Ocean

The first symbol of the US naval strategy in the Indian Ocean was witnessed when in December 1971, the aircraft carrier 'Enterprise' and its task force entered the Bay of Bengal. It was the time when Bangladesh war was going on. It was a tragedy that on the day the UN passed the resolution on 16 December 1971 calling upon all powers to treat the Indian Ocean as a zone of peace, the US Seventh Fleet entered the Bay of Bengal for reasons which were far from being peace oriented. The task force remained in the Indian Ocean till 10 January 1972.

The matter did not end there. The US announced a programme of sending a task force to the Indian Ocean every few months. Subsequently a seventh fleet task force consisting of an aircraft carrier 'Hancock' and five destroyers entered the Indian Ocean through the straits of Malacca on 29 October 1973. The plea given was the usual one: the continuing Soviet build-up in the Mediterranean. Again on 30 November 1973 and later in December another US naval force headed by the aircraft carrier 'Oriskeny' and subsequently reinforced by the nuclear power guided missiles carrying frigate 'Bainbridge' entered the Indian Ocean. It was almost on the day when Brezhnev addressed the Indian Parliament on 29 November

1973 and the joint Indo-Soviet declaration proposing Indian Ocean a zone of peace was issued that Americans took this step. In March 1974, the more modern aircraft carrier 'Kitty Hawk' was sent with the instructions that it would stay up to the reopening of the Suez.

By the agreement signed in 1972, the US government gained rights to establish what was officially called 'a communication facility in Diego Garcia as part of its global network. The facility as was being utilised since April 1973 comprised a small airstrip, a communication station and some 200 naval personnel to operate the vessels at their disposal.[1] The US defence department, which since October 1973 West Asian war decided to maintain a regular naval presence in the Indian Ocean, wanted to expand the existing facility into a regular naval complex from which its naval and air units could monitor activity in the western and southern approaches of the Indian Ocean as well as protect the oil lanes that led from the Persian Gulf. Before negotiating this deal, the US maintained a small naval unit in Baharain. As Baharain was going to terminate its agreement with the US later in 1974 and as there was possibility of fuel supplies for its ships from Arab sources to be discontinued indefinitely, the US apparently regarded Diego Garcia as a viable alternative. Diego Garcia which could act as a stationery air craft carrier right in the middle of the Indian Ocean could also relieve the US of the necessity to maintain a costly floating carrier force with all the logistic problems that it would pose.[2]

When the Pentagon asked the Congress to sanction $20 million for expanding Diego Garcia, some members raised their voice against the project on the ground that there was no point in America playing the role of a policeman in the region where they had no involvement. Secondly, when the US was reducing its military presence abroad, a new base in Indian Ocean could start a chain reaction for additional bases to support it—Diego Garcia today and some Indonesian port tomorrow. Thirdly the move would further stimulate a US-Soviet naval race in the Indian Ocean and elsewhere. Finally, it would be frustrating to the Indian Ocean littoral states which wished to keep the area demilitarised.[3] Instead, some Congressmen suggested that the US and the Soviet Union should come together and work for a detente and a general arms limitation agreement.

These objections could not deter the powerful naval lobby in the Pentagon. Their spokesman J.M. Cain, Commander of the US Pacific Fleet said that a port in American control in Indian Ocean was as important as Malta in the Mediterranean. In his view it was the nerve centre of Indian Ocean extremely important strategically. The US nuclear submarines based in Diego Garcia, would have as their aim the entire south Asian continent, eastern part of Africa and west Asia thus dominating the entire Indian Ocean region. Moreover, far removed as it was from other countries of Asia and Africa, the base activities in Diego Garcia would have no impact on the national public opinion of any of the countries of the region. That is why the Americans were evacuating their bases from Bahrain. No country would blame the US for occupying a territory which belonged to some of them. But by being there the US would maintain its indirect presence in the Indian Ocean. Strategically, it would be an important linking point in the chain of naval bases from those located near south east coast of Africa to the Australian controlled Cocoa islands. This would link together the Atlantic and Pacific military systems.

As regards India's stand on this issue, the common American belief has been that India had aligned itself with the Soviet Union in opposing the American moves in the Indian Ocean. According to their belief, the Indian Parliament could not afford to allocate sufficient funds to provide a significantly greater role for the navy so long as the main threat to India's security was by land. That fact added to western concern of India being made dependent on Soviet naval power especially in the event of an increased sense of maritime threat from China. Some Americans also believed that their presence in Indian Ocean was justified in terms of the growing Russian presence in the area and India's nuclear test. In this context, a question was posed: would Diego Garcia be used for a pre-emptive strike against India if it opted for military nuclear programme?[4] This appeared to be a fanciful thinking but the American moves in the Indian Ocean and the arguments in support thereof had created so much distrust and suspicion among the Indian people that such questions became quite common.

The general impression among almost all the littoral states was that whatever may have been the American motive in occupying Diego Garcia their main aim was to maintain their own international potential in the area and to acquire the military and diplomatic leverage that it could enjoy in influencing all coastal states. Moreover, it could hardly be believed that the US aim in having bases in Indian Ocean was only to oppose the Soviet presence as the US had a vast net work of bases and its ships enjoyed the right of moorage and refuelling in ports of South Africa, Australia and other countries. The obvious object appeared to be to control international trade routes which passed through these regions and to exert pressure on coastal states rich in oil and other natural resources.[5] It is because of such apprehensions that this policy evoked an international chorus of protests from nations in the region including India, Sri Lanka and two of America's closest allies Australia and New Zealand.

The External Affairs Minister, Swaran Singh made it clear that India did not want to view this issue in its bilateral context with the United States when an overwhelming number of littoral countries were opposed to the establishment of bases and arms build-up in the Indian Ocean.[6] Power rivalry was not an issue which exclusively concerned India. India's persistent criticism annoyed many Americans, one of them being the American ambassador Moynihan who went to the extent of suggesting that the Indian Ocean be named Madagascar sea. Indian spokesman pointed out that it was a fact of geography and not a gift of the US government.[7]

In India, it was often asked whether it was the presence of American Polaris submarines that attracted the Soviet navy to the Indian Ocean or whether the growth of Russian influence and interest in the area had obliged the US to pay greater attention to it than in the past. The American spokesman often briefed the Indians to equate their presence in the Indian Ocean with the Soviet positions in the neighbouring region. The American ambassador Goheen on 10 September 1977 said at Madras that his country could not give up the Diego Garcia bases unless the Soviet Union gave up Berbara in Somalia. But later when the Soviet Union was forced to leave Berbara, the US continued to retain their hold on Diego Garcia. The Indian viewpoint that super power rivalry in the Indian Ocean also constituted threat to security to India, did not carry much weight with the US policy-makers.[8]

The US had no objection to any country in the Indian Ocean which might require the presence within quick-call of a sizeable segment of its naval and air power. It had in fact calculatedly armed Iran to assume the responsibility of maintaining regional stability and protecting the various Sheikhdoms against any domestic or foreign threat.[9] Finally, the Nixon doctrine which was still the administration's accepted policy clearly ruled out any direct US military role in the area. The best course would have been that the US negotiated with the Soviet Union about what would be the naval limits in the Indian Ocean and elsewhere.

Indo-US differences on this issue continued to persist though India tried several times to plead with American leadership to realise how their involvement in the region would cause super power rivalry and disturb the peace of the region. At the initiative of several littoral states, including India a proposal was made to convene an international conference in Colombo in 1981 where well-meaning efforts would be undertaken to find a formula acceptable to both the super powers to make this region a zone of peace.

India was really concerned at the reluctance of the US administration which by implication questioned the motives of the sponsors of the conference. The conference was postponed to 1985 largely due to the US and its allies' insistence that the 1971 UN resolution be 'harmonised' so as to take into account the Soviet intervention in Afghanistan. India did not agree with this pre-condition as it was unnecessarily tagged to the crisis in Afghanistan. To India it appeared to be a complex issue caused by the conflicting policies of several countries including China, USA and USSR with which regional countries like Iran and Pakistan had also aligned to serve their ends.[10] However, the plan to hold the conference could not materialize and the proposal remained on the international agenda.

## China Factor

It may be recalled that during the Chinese aggression in 1962, the US tried to pressure India to accept the recommendations of Harriman–Sandys mission which suggested that India should give-up the Kashmir valley to Pakistan in order to fight China over the sparsely populated Ladakh frontier. Since the Janata take over in 1977, the US officials continued to persuade India to normalise relations with China in this respect. In American views this accommodation should be on the basis of giving up the territory already under Chinese occupation. That is India would have to give up its claim to Indian territory in Ladakh occupied by China.[11]

It was doubtful whether the US had similarly advised China to make concessions to India which amounted to restoration of the land that the Chinese had occupied during the aggression period; in brief, to restore the status quo as it existed before the commencement of aggression. These suggestions were made when the Chinese radio in its broadcasts on 27th November 1977 made references to their border dispute with India, Soviet Union and Vietnam. It said: 'on 20 October 1962, the Indian reactionaries launched an all out massive attack on our border guards. On Tibet and Sinkiang frontiers, our units were forced to fire back in self-defence. In a little more than a month, they completely smashed the Indian army's full scale offensive and dismantled all their military strong holds built on Chinese territory. It also said that it was the Chinese government that took the initiative in bringing about a ceasefire, releasing all prisoners of war and returning large quantities of captured war material. With such a China the USA wanted India to come to terms.

Again in 1962, in the wake of Chinese aggression the US administration gave us some arms. But it had not been realised by many that China's attack itself was partly prompted by the US provocation in Tibet through Indian air space. Taking advantage of the 1962 situation, the US tried to impose an unfavourable solution of Kashmir problem and also install a Voice of America transmitter in India. When the Government of India found neither of these proposals acceptable the arms aid came to a stop.[12]

Despite Nehru's appeal for air protection, President Kennedy could not do much for reasons which were said to be in the larger interests of India. But the US in its own strategic interests, which they felt would coincide with India's security requirements, installed nuclear power monitoring instrument in Nanda Devi mountains to record Chinese rocket telementry and atomic tests.[13]

**Vietnam**

Indian people were shocked over the US aggression on Vietnam particularly the savage bombing resulting in mass destruction of men and material. Mrs. Gandhi was reported to have said at the One Asia Assembly that whether that sort of war or brutal bombing which had taken place in Vietnam would have been tolerated for so long had the people been Europeans.[14] The Vietnam war was a traumatic experience of the Vietnamese, no doubt. It had been a laboratory for experimenting new weapons and it had been on a scale of aerial bombardment unknown in history.[15] The irony of the situation was that Mrs. Gandhi's comments came a day after Moynihan, ambassador designate to India had told the Senate foreign relations committee that Mrs. Gandhi and President

Nixon had exchanged notes secretly and that US-India relations seemed to be improving. Moynihan's appointment suggested that Nixon was trying to heal the rift with Mrs. Gandhi.

The US administration took strong exception to Mrs. Gandhi's remarks and rumours were that Moynihan may postpone his departure to India. The official spokesman said that Mrs. Gandhi's statement contradicted the recent communication from India suggesting a desire to improve relations between the two countries. Mrs. Gandhi had also earlier criticised the US policy in Vietnam but the latest statement came as something of a surprise.[16] This time her remarks were an indirect accusation of the US for having waged a racial war in Indo-China. Though the statement did not mention the US by name, the official view was that their remarks were directed at the US.

India was not the only country to raise its voice against American war in Vietnam. Olaf Palme, Prime Minister of Sweden, had also made similar remarks and they were treated with harsh rejoinders. The Secretary of State, Rogers was particularly angry with the 'gratuitous statements' of the Swede Premier; he took strong exception to the comparison that the Olaf had made between the Nazi atrocities in Europe with American savagery in Vietnam. Nixon had ordered the US charge d'affaires in Stockholm who was then in Washington for consultation not to go back to resume his duty there. He also told the Swede government not to send their envoy to Washington in a hurry.[17] Nixon was reported to have asked his senior officials not to socialise with the spokesmen of Sweden and eleven other nations blacklisted for their audacity in criticising US policies in Vietnam. It may be recalled here that the brusque postponement by President Johnson of Lal Bahadur Shastri's visit to the US in June 1965 provided a parallel. The date for the visit had been fixed at Washington's initiative. Despite this undignified step Indian government emphatically reiterated that India's policy on Vietnam would remain unchanged. It was believed in certain diplomatic circles in Washington that Mrs. Gandhi might have been led to say what she did because she wanted to compensate for the restraints with which India reacted when the actual bombing was in progress in December and when even close allies of the US were using strong words.[18]

It was true that Nixon inherited the Vietnam war from his predecessor but he could not be forgiven for having carried it out for four years in a most ruthless manner. He felt offended when he was reminded of his guilt by well meaning friends of the US. As regards the timing of Mrs. Gandhi's statement, it would have been an abdication of responsibility on her part if in addressing a gathering which called itself one Asia Assembly she had not referred to a matter of the great interest and concern to the whole continent. It would have also been a sign of weakness on her part if she had not given expression to the wide spread sentiment that such things as had happened in Vietnam would never have been permitted for so long in a European country. It was also a warning that Indo-US friendship could not be built on New Delhi's acquiescence in Washington's action which it regarded as morally reprehensible and against America's own best interests.

The mini crisis seemed to have been ended when Mrs. Gandhi in her statement in Kathmandu on 8 February said that her sharply critical remarks about Vietnam were not aimed at any particular country. This, to some extent, mollified the American administration. Kenneth Bush, Deputy Secretary of State said they had received and accepted with satisfaction Mrs. Gandhi's statement in Kathmandu. They had differences with great democracy—India, before and would probably have other, from time to time but he felt sure that as the time passed they would reach higher plateau of understanding.[19]

**Refuelling Facilities**

During the Gulf war, the Chandra Sekhar government allowed American transport planes to refuel in India on their way to the war theatre. This was interpreted in some political circle as being a violation of the diplomatic principle of neutrality towards belligerents in a war to which India was not a party. The government contention was that India was not neutral in this war but was very much part of it. As it was a war authorised by the UN through the Security Council resolution, which India did not oppose, it was obligatory on its part to go by the UN decision. The trouble appeared to have been that the US had converted what was supposed to be a war by the UN into virtually an American war.[20]

The provisions of the UN Charter, under which this war was authorised, made it compulsory for any UN member to assist in the war when called upon to do so, although of course, the sovereignty of member nations placed some limit upon what could be demanded of them. But granting refuelling rights did not violate these limits in any way and in fact to refuse the Americans to refuel their planes would have violated India's obligations to the UN.[21]

Iraq had annexed Kuwait, another Arab country, a member of the UN and NAM, that had helped it in its war against Iran. This Iraqi action was regarded as a most indefensible aggression to resist which was the objective of all justice loving countries. India could not contribute any thing in money or material terms. Indian permission to refuel American planes was a small contribution to reverse the invasion militarily against Kuwait since Iraq had refused to accept peaceful withdrawal of its troops from the Kuwait territory. It was well understood that the UN resolution authorised action only for evicting Iraq from Kuwait and not for destroying Iraq or its military capabilities or for imposing upon the West Asia region a regime devised by the US for its own purposes.[22] Financially also it was not going to cost much to India as the US command had agreed to pay landing fees and to replace the fuel that would be supplied to the American planes.

The opposition parties demanded immediate suspension of over flights and refuelling facilities to military air crafts of foreign countries who were involved in the West Asian war.[23] The Congress party, in particular warned that they would not allow 'our vital national interests to be diluted'. To the opponents it amounted to indirect help to US war efforts in the Gulf region. To them it was a deviation from the country's consistent policy of non alignment and anti-imperialism. A significant point made was that India's capacity to intervene in the Gulf war for a peaceful and political solution of the problem had been eroded by the government taking such a step.

The war had its origin in the dispute between Iraq and Kuwait on the over production of crude by Kuwait beyond its quota which slumped down its prices in international market causing serious losses to the oil producing countries including Iraq. It was forgotten that with Kuwait in his pocket Saddam could control 19 per cent of the World's oil and had he taken Saudi Arabia, he would have ended up with 44 per cent of the World's oil.[24] The Government of India, in the opinion of the opponents, had lost sight of the real cause of the war.

As regards the American reactions, contrary to the expectations in some quarters there was no open expression of resentment by the Bush administration because it appreciated the fact that India with the policy of nonalignment and a big muslim population was under severe compulsion to take a particular line of action. They felt that India helped them at a critical moment and they wanted to respect its sensitivities at a difficult juncture to its domestic politics.[25]

## REFERENCES

1. *Hindu*, 23 January 1974 from Easwar Sagar

2. Ibid

3. Ibid, 12 February 1974

4. Hirnmay Karlekar, 'The Indian Ocean: How to prevent big power rivalry *Statesmen*, 3 December 1974

5. K.L. Frost in *Motherland*, 17 March 1974, also *National Herald*, 17 March 1974

6. IDSA News Review on North-America and Europe 1974, p. 1087
7. *Hindustan Times*, 7 March 1974
8. *Mainstream*, 31 December 1977, p. 31
9. *Hindustan Times*, 8 February 1974 from Krishan Bhatia
10. Ibid
11. *Mainstream*, 31 December 1977, p. 31
12. K.R. Malkani in *Times of India*, 15 April 1985
13. Sunanda K. Dutt Ray, 'India and the USA' in the *Statesman*, 3 February 1991
14. Bernard Weinvauh in *International Herald Tribune*, 7 February 1974
15. *National Herald*, 9 February 1974
16. *Times of India*, 9 September 1973
17. *Hindu*, 9 February 1973 from Easwar Sagar in Washington
18. *Times of India*, 10 February 1973 edit: US Petulence
19. *Hindu*, 11 February 1973 from Easwar Sagar in Washington
20. Pran Chopra, *The Crisis in Foreign Policy*, p. 219
21. Ibid
22. Ibid., 181
23. V.D. Chopra in *Patriot*, 3 February 1991
24. Talveen Singh in *Indian Express*, 21 January 1971
25. *Times of India*, 6 August 1991 from T.R. Menon in Washington

# 13

# Concluding Observations

It has been a well understood assumption that a love-hate relationship such as existed between India and the US was inevitable in the circumstances in which the two countries had to interact towards each other. Both sides seemed to be helpless in deviating from a certain course each adopted for reasons of its own. India, for instance, in following the dictates of non-alignment had often to take a line of action which was not to the liking of the American leaders who went to the extent of calling it opportunistic or immoral. The US, on the other hand as a champion of democratic values, supported dictatorships and autocratic regimes in several countries on the ground that the administrative stability that they provided held out the promise of orderly development within the necessary discipline. They remained stubborn in sticking to what they considered an article of faith for them. Thus the two countries for most of the time continued to talk from different wave lengths, like two persons standing on opposite sides of a wide chasm calling at each other but neither catching the message of the other. In brief, it turned out to be a dialogue of the deaf.

After the end of Bangladesh war in December 1971, there seemed to be a genuine desire in India and Pakistan to normalise their mutual relations. Chinese were also quiet having reconciled to the inevitability of the emergence of

Bangladesh as an independent state. But sometimes prejudices die hard. In certain political circles in American society, doubts continued to linger about India's bonafides in restoring peace in the subcontinent. The Assistant Secretary of State, Sisco warned India that they would regard any new threat to Pakistan's integrity as disruption to the progress towards peace and stability in South Asia.[1]

When Bangladesh applied for membership to the UN in the middle of 1972, Pakistan and China urged that the question be deferred till Bangladesh had complied with the General Assembly resolutions of 7 and 21 October 1971. The US supported India's proposal for the immediate entry of Bangladesh into the UN. China cast its first veto in the Security Council on 25 August 1973 barring Bangladesh's entry into the world body.[2] Later, the three way repatriation agreement between India, Pakistan and Bangladesh in August 1973 cleared the way for a balanced approach by the big powers to the subcontinent. The agreement which envisaged an early recognition of Bangladesh by Pakistan left no excuse for China to oppose any longer Bangladesh's admission to the UN. The agreement was supposed to eliminate the Pakistan syndrome from the process of normalisation of Indo-US relations which had remained strained since the Bangladesh crisis.

A good idea of the improvement in India's relations with the US could be had from the agreement of Washington to release development grant of $ 87.6 million which remained impounded since 1971.[3] It was further witnessed by the sharp increase in the Aid Consortium assistance to India which was demonstrated by the fact that gross net commitment earmarked for India increased from $ 948 million in 1972-73 to $ 1860 million in 1974-75.[4] The agreement signed in 1973 on the settlement of the rupee accumulation arising from the PL 480 wheat sale to India removed a long standing source of friction between the two countries.

Again under the pressure of Pak lobby, the US decided in mid-1973 to resume arms supply to Pakistan. But Nixon in his May 1973 report announced that only the non-lethal weapons would be supplied to India and Pakistan subject to the condition that arms supplied to Pakistan would form part of their aid programme to that country whereas those given to India would be on commercial basis.

India's nuclear test on 17 May 1974 further created tension in some American circles. The American ambassador in India Daniel Patrick Moynihan in a meeting with Mrs. Gandhi stated the US reactions which warned India that this event may encourage Pakistan to develop its nuclear weapon making capability. He clearly said that in a decade's time some Pakistani General may call up and say he had few nuclear weapons in hand on the strength of which he could claim Kashmir.[5] In such a contingency both the countries would be in mortal danger of unleashing a nuclear war. The American envoy felt that as a big power it was India's responsibility to take initiative to see that such a situation of confrontation did never arise.

The visit of Kissinger in October 1974, resulted in the establishment of a Indo-US joint commission on economic, educational and scientific cooperation. It was during this visit that the Indian Prime Minister invited the American President to visit India some time next year. The main achievement of Kissinger's visit was the impression he left behind that the new Indo-US understanding he had established was not a fragile one man's accomplishment but something that could become the cornerstone of future US policies in South Asian region.[6]

Trends towards improvement in Indo-US relations continued to be perceptible even after Kissinger's departure. In June 1975 Foreign Minister Y.B. Chavan declared that the time had come to go ahead with establishing a more mature relationship between the two countries. This statement did not go unnoticed among the Americans. Within days, ambassador Saxbe told a meeting of the Indo-American group in New York that Chavan's statement was the signal they had been waiting for.[7]

A few days later when the emergency was declared, Kissinger asked all the US officials to refrain from commenting on internal developments in India. For its part, India made a friendly gesture to the US by reversing its stand on Cuba's move in the UN to have the US Caribbean territory of Puerto Rico inscribed on the UN agenda as a colony yet to be liberated and by voting for its postponement.[8]

The hopeful trends in Indo-US relations witnessed after Kissinger's visit received a setback in February 1975 when the US resumed arms supplies to Pakistan. In addition to the protest officially lodged it was also announced that Y.B. Chavan would not attend the meeting of Indo-US joint commission that was going to be held in Washington in March that year.

The Carter administration was less abrasive and arrogant in its dealings with India but it did not make any major departure from the erstwhile policies of the previous administration. Foreign policy was not a major issue in the Presidential election since the whole thrust of the Carter campaign was to clean the cobwebs of Watergate scandal. The new administration took a more realistic attitude towards arms sales to Pakistan, it was much tougher on other issues such as the supply of nuclear equipment even for peaceful purposes. His annoyance with Morarji Desai's insistence on sticking to Indian policy on nuclear issue was well known particularly on his refusal to sign the NPT. This he wanted to express in a tough and blunt note which he proposed to send to Morarji on his return to Washington.

There was no illusion in India of any dramatic change in the American policies towards India, though some change for the better was perceptible in the general attitude of the administration. Indian people tended to look upon the Democrats as much more friendly and sympathetic lot than the Republicans but it was also true that the liberal elements in the Democratic party had been more critical of India than their Republican counterparts.

In this context it should be noted that the US foreign policy has been by and large, a bilateral policy with a strong element of continuity in it. It has been a far more institutionalised policy in so far as both the Democrats and Republicans subscribed to the basic themes of US global responsibilities and interests. It is on the projection and application of these themes that they differed at times not on the substance of the policy pursued in terms of its international commitments.

In October 1977 three somewhat significant events in Indo-US relations took place which infused hope in both countries to improve their mutual relations. First was the announcement of the visit of President Carter to India in the last week of November 1977 but which actually took place in January 1978; second was the appointment of an eminent jurist, Nani Palkhiwala as India's ambassador to the US which the administration regarded as a gesture to the recognition of their diplomatic eminence, and lastly, the External Affairs Minister Atal Behari Vajpayee's visit to the annual session of the UN General Assembly during which period he met several US dignitaries.

During the Afghan crisis, the US joined hands with China in providing military aid to Pakistan. Not only the earlier suspension was revoked, some more assistance was given, to enable Pakistan to repel invasion. What worried India more was the swift manner in which arms aid worth $ 3.2 billion was given to Pakistan in 1981 not to counter a possible Soviet expansion towards Pakistan but to face a similar threat from India. This is what Alexander Haig, Secretary of State clearly admitted mincing no words to leave anybody in doubt.[9]

Mrs. Gandhi tried to read the Afghan situation quite differently which did not please the Americans. She made a three point statement: *(i)* what happened in Afghanistan was an internal affairs in which no outside power should have interfered ; *(ii)* Soviet troops were there at the invitation of the government which repeated more strongly the appeal made by the previous government of Hafizullah Amin, *(iii)* those who criticised Soviet intervention did not utter a word of protest against the Chinese intervention in Vietnam in February 1979.[10]

She felt that the crisis in Afghanistan did not develop with the entry of the Soviet troops but with the US efforts to create the tension of cold war in the region after the fall of the Shah of Iran. The government stance on this issue was explained as follows, *(i)* India's stand did not mean support to the Soviet intervention, *(ii)* in India's perception the rearming of Pakistan by the US and China and the extension of super power confrontation in the region were more destabilising for the whole area than what had happened in Afghanistan earlier. *(iii)* The main thrust of India's diplomacy was to defuse the crisis and damn the confrontation.

In October 1981, Mrs. Gandhi and Reagan met at Cancun Mexico, during a summit meeting of heads of government of a few industrialised countries and developing nations to review the prospects of creating a new international economic order. Though the summit did not achieve much, the contacts between heads did create an atmosphere of understanding in which India and the US would make some headway towards better relations. The process had begun in the form of increased bilateral trade, increase in diplomatic dialogue and the military to military contacts. One factor that helped the process was that the US had largely accomplished its goals in Afghanistan, though India never accepted continued Pakistan's involvement in Afghanistan that had the support of the US. However that phase had passed and a new one started. Friendly relations do not grow quickly after years of estrangement.

In May 1990, Indo-Pak relations deteriorated over the growing incursions of Islamabad-backed militants in Kashmir. President Bush sent two of his senior officers, Robert Gats, deputy national security adviser and John Kelly acting Secretary of State to the subcontinent. American observers believed that as a result of their frankly telling the leaders of the two countries that any fresh clash in Kashmir would lead to a nuclear war, which could be a mortal danger for both of them, the possibility of nuclear confrontation was averted.[11]

Besides the official interactions, the annual Indo-American bilateral strategic dialogue organised by IDSA and Washington based National Defence University served as a major effort to remove mutual misperceptions and enhance understanding among the strategic communities in both the countries. Another development witnessed during Bush administration in 1991 was the enhanced level of defence cooperation between the two countries, the military to military interaction between the American and Indian armed forces had consistently risen, particularly in the fields of joint consultation and training of officers, also the navies of the two countries had started holding joint exercises in the Indian Ocean.[12]

It seemed that the future relationship between India and the US in the post-cold war era would depend on how each country viewed the other. The US administration had been quite sensitive to endorse certain actions India took in defence of its national interests such as sending Indian army to quell the rebellion against the authorities in Maldives and similar action in Sri Lanka in an effort to bring about reconciliation between the fighting forces of Sri Lanka government and Tamil Liberation Front. This amounted to giving limited support to the concept of regional hegemony. But this applied where the US interests were not involved; it actually meant the preservation of the status quo.

The case of Pakistan was different as there the American interests were vitally affected. Pakistan is located in a region which is geographically linked with China, Russia and above all, the entire Arab world. By keeping Pakistan appeased the US seeks to meet its several diplomatic ends. The US policy had been directed towards the support of regional solution of regional problems so far its national interests remained safe and unaffected. In the Indian subcontinent, the Americans put their weight behind the Simla agreement and the confidence building measures but what unfortunately had come in the way was their policy of escalating arms race between India and Pakistan. This has been a chronic problem which remained unsolved till today.

## REFERENCES

1. John W. Mellor, *India, a Rising Middle Power*, p. 133.
2. *Hindustan Times*, 26 August 1972
3. *Times of India,* 16 March 1973
4. *Economic and Political Weekly,* 18 October 1975, p. 1631
5. Dinesh Kumar, *Defence in India, US Cooperation*, p. 28.
6. *Hindu*, 31 October 1974 from G.K. Reddy
7. *Economic and Political Weekly*, 18 October 1974, p. 1631
8. Ibid
9. *Times of India,* 1 July 1981
10. *Indian Express*, 23 January 1980
11. *New York Times*, *Washington* Post 16 May 1990 Cited in C. Mahapatra, *Indo-US Relations in the 21st Century*, p. 44.
12. Ibid. 109.

# Index

Accord of Afghanistan, 6, 7
Afghan Crisis, 43-53, 74, 82, 92, 102, 105, 148
  After Soviet withdrawal, 83
  Carter on, 43-44
  Carter policy pursued by Reagan, 44
  CIA supply weapons to Afghan rebels, 45
  Clifford visit to India, 50
  Indian diplomatic forays, 51-52
  Issue refereed to Security Council, 46, 51
  Soviet forces bound to leave, 92
  Soviet intervention took place India, 46-52
  Soviet occupation created threat to Iran and Pakistan, 43-44
  Soviet troop in Afghanistan, 43, 90, 149
  US aid to Mujahideans, 44-45
  US not prepared to a direct war with Soviet Union, 45-46
Afghanistan, 6
Agni, 105-06
Ahmad, Fakhruddin Ali, 25
Aid India Consortium, 29, 145
Akash, 106
Albert, Carl, 25
Alexander, PC, 80
American arms aid threat to India, 101-02
American atomic scientists visited Tarapur, 112
American interest in Pakistan, 150
American policies, 2
American policy of arms parity between India and Pakistan, 88-90
American victory in Gulf War, 7
Amin, Hafizullah, 148
Anschluss of Austria, 18
Anti-India lobbies in US Congress, 106
Anti tank warfare, 78
Arjun tank, 82
Armitage Richard, 65, 105
Armscost, Michael, 81
Asian Development Bank, 58
Atomic power plant at Tarapur, 111
AWACS, 91-92

Bain bridge, 132
Bangladesh, 14
Bangladesh crisis in 1971, 2, 9-12, 144-45
  Alienation between India and USA, 9
  Break-up of Pakistan, 11
  Caused tension in Indo-US relations, 11
  China and US reconciled, 12
  Efforts initiated by US, 4, 9-10

India announced ceasefire, 9-11
Refugee problem, 2
Soviet pressure on USA, 9-10
US opposed India for, 11

Bangladesh for UN membership, 145
Bangladesh liberation war, 99
Barness, Harry G, 91
Bhagat, BR, 84
Bhandari, Romesh, 74
Bhutto, ZA, 14, 21, 88
Brazil, 125
Brezezinsky, 35, 101
Brezhnev, Leonid, 43, 51, 132
Buckley, James, 90
Burns, Kenneth, 103
Visit to India, 103

Bush, George, 61-63, 91-92, 106, 125-26, 142, 150
Visit to India, 61-63, 91

Bush, Kenneth, 140

Cain, JM, 134
Cartucco, Frank, 104
Carter enquired about health of Jaya Prakash Narayan, 1
Carter, Jimmy, 1, 5, 26, 28, 30, 36, 37-38, 43-44, 46-47, 54, 61, 89, 94, 100, 113-15, 120, 147
Carter on Indo-Pak relations, 5
Carter visit to India, 5, 30-36, 148
Chandra Shekhar, 8, 140
Charan Singh, 46-48
Chavan, YB, 21, 23-24, 89, 146-47
Children style, 119
China, 3-4, 6, 23, 37
China factor, 137-38
Chinese bomb blast, 17
Chou En-lai, 11
Christopher, Warren, 29, 89, 101
CIA, 4, 44-45, 101, 106
Civil liberties, 5
Clifford visit to India, 50
Commonwealth Prime Ministers Conference, 80
Comprehensive nuclear ban treaty, 32
Connolly, John B, 14
Meet Mrs. Gandhi, 14

Cronin, Richard, 64
Cuban forces in Africa, 37
Cyrus Vance, 28

Defence Cooperation, 99-108
Advanced weapon technology for India, 103
American duel use technology, 104
India purchased arms from US, 100-02
Steps towards developing military ties, 104
US arms supply to Pakistan after Bangladesh, 99-100
US contribution marginal, 99
US force all deals with India, 99

Democratic Party, 79
Desai, Morarji, 1, 5, 28-31, 34-35, 36-41, 61, 100-01, 110, 114, 147
Visit to USA, 5-6, 36-41, 115

Diego Garcia, 20, 133-36
Dulles, 91

Economic and Scientific interactions, 118-31
American blocked rupee accounts, 118-19
Bilateral trade, 122-26
India did not like approaching US for economic aid, 118

Reaction to Bangladesh War, US aid suspended, 118

Resumption of direct US aid to India, 119

Rupee debt agreement, 119

Science and technology, 126-29

Uneasiness caused by Afghan crisis, 120

US development aid to India, 120-21

US reduce contribution to UN, 128-29

Eisenhover, 91

Emergency proclamation, 21-26

Enriched uranium shipment for Tarapur, 38-39, 49, 54, 58, 111, 115

Ford, 16-17, 20-21, 24, 26, 28, 101

Called off visit for to India, 22-23M

Gandhi, Indira, 4, 7, 10, 13, 18, 22-25, 48, 50-52, 119-20, 127, 129, 138-40, 148

Come back, 54, 59

Death of, 65-66

Defeat of, 29

Pro-Soviet policy, 24

Visit to Canada, 16

Visit to Moscow, 56

Visit to USA, 56, 60, 116

Gandhi, Rajiv, 7-8, 65-68, 91, 110, 127

In office, 70-85

Visit to Moscow, 74

Visit to USA, 71-78, 102, 110

Gats, Roberts, 149

Generalised system of preference, 122

Geneva accord on Afghanistan, 92

Germany, 7, 61

Glenn, John, 68, 95

Goa, 2, 18

Goheen, 136

Gonslave, Eric, 51-52

Goodwill between Desai and Carter, 1

Gorbachev, Michael, 74, 92

Gromyko, Andrei, 52, 60

Gulf War, 7-8, 107, 140, 142

Haig, Alexander, 148

Hancock, 132

Harpoon missiles, 78

Harriman Sandys mission, 137

Hawkaye airborne radar system, 78

Hi-tech trade, 76

Hollen, Christopher, 19

House of Representative Committee on International Relations, 39-40

Huang Hua of China, 10, 51

Ikle, Fred, 103, 128

IMF, 7, 55

Indian Atomic Energy Commission, 55

Indian Ocean, 3, 10, 20, 107, 132,-37, 150

Zone of peace, 133

India Pakistan relations, 1, 5, 151

India-US shared democratic values, 2

India's aspiration to use nuclear energy, 3

India's efforts to improve relations with China, 3

India's efforts to improve relations with Soviet Unions, 3

India's missile programme, 106

India's nuclear explosion, 17

India's nuclear test, 146

India's reaction to dowing South Korean civil airliner by Soviet missile, 59-60

Indira Gandhi's come back, 54-69
- After Mrs. Gandhi, 64-68
- Indira visit to USA, 56
- Regular contacts between Indian leaders, 59-61
- Soviet intervention in Afghanistan, 54
- Strains in Indo-US relations, 55-56
- US administration set aside India's contention that Pakistan was no threat from Soviet, 54
- Visit to Moscow, 56-57

Indira-Reagan met at Cancun Maxico, 149
Indira-Reagan talks, 60
Indo-American bilateral strategic dialogue, 150
Indo-Soviet relations, 5
Indo-Soviet treaty, 17, 20
Indo-US Business Council, 41
Indo-US Joint Commission, 23, 146
Indo-US relations, 1-8
- Improvement in, 146
- Love-hate relationship, 145
- Motives of goodwill, 1
- Positive phase of, 2-3
- Psychological factors, 3
- Significant events in, 148
- Strained since Bangladesh crisis, 4

Indo-US Sub Commission on Science, 129
International Atomic Energy Agency, 113-14
International Development Association fund India's share of, 29
International Executive service Corps, 41
Israel, 37-38

**J**agaur strike aircrafts, 100
Janata Regime, 28-42, 100, 114
- American people and media welcomed by, 28
- Carter decision to end earlier tilt towards Pakistan, 29
- Carter visit, 30-36
- Statement of goodwill, 29

Japan. 7
Jay Prakash Narayan, 1
Jhonson, 139
Joint Indo-US efforts to bring Arjun tanks, 82

**K**alb Barnard, 72
Kamath, MV, 25
Karnal, Babrak, 43
Kashmir, 2, 8, 76, 137, 149
Kaul, TN, 26
Kelly, John, 149
Kennedy, 138
Khomenie, Ayatollah, 43, 83
Kickleighter, Clark, 107
Kissinger, Henry, 9-10, 15-16, 24, 28, 87-89, 146-47
- Visit to India, 18-21, 100, 146

Klaein, Herbert, 14
Kreps, Juanila, 41
Kuwait. 142
Kyle, 16

**L**adakh, 137
Lake placid, 16
Lindstrom, Talbot, 103
- Visit to India, 103

**M**adagascar, 135
Maldives, 105
Merger of Sikkim, 17-18

Military transport aircrafts, 107-08
Mishra, SN, 46
Mohawk battlefield, 78
Moynihan, P, 20, 88, 135, 138-39, 146
Mujahaddin rebeals, 84
Mukherji, Pranab, 120
Murphy, Richard, 64, 102, 105
  Visit to India, 64, 102
Mutual Development and Cooperation Act, 118

Najibullah, 82-83
NAM summit, 60, 141
Narasimha Rao, PV, 56, 58, 91
NATO, 90
Nehru, Jawaharlal, 7, 71, 138
Nicargua, 84
Nixon, 2, 9-10, 14-17, 87, 136, 139-40, 145
Nixon Breznev summit, 16
Nixon's birthday message to Mrs.. Gandhi, 15
Nixon tilt towards Pakistan, 20
Non proliferation, 30, 40
NRC, 112-15
  Shipment of enriched uranium, 115
Nuclear energy for war purposes India would not use of, 5
Nuclear factor, 109-17
  India's refusal to treaty, 110
  Nuclear fuel issue, 111-117
  Nuclear weapon powers, 110
  Proliferation, 109
  US appeals India on NPT, 113
  US pressure, 110
Nuclear fuel, 39, 111-117
Nuclear issue, 33, 38-39
Nuclear proliferation Act, 34, 39, 97, 109
Nuclear Proliferation treaty, 3, 39-40, 106, 109-11, 147
Nuclear weapon race, 94
Nunn, Sam, 67-68
Nunn visit to India, 67-68
Nye, Joseph, 114

Oriskeny, 132

Pak army defeat in Bangladesh, 93
Pakistan, 1-3, 20-21, 38, 73
Pakistan factor, 86-98
  Carter disapprove sale of US A-7 fighter to, 89
  Carter revived policy on Soviet intervention in Afghanistan to, 90-92
  Cold War, 86
  India concern, 86
  Indian opposition to resumption of arms supplies to, 88-91
  Indo-Pak war in 1965, 87
  Pakistan ally of US, 86
  Pakistan ensure protection of US interest in South Asia, 106
  US arms supplies to, 87-88
Pakistan involvement in Afghanistan, 149
Pakistan nuclear policy US support, 93-97
Pak prisoners of war, 14
Palestinian Liberation Organisation, 76
Palkhiwala, Nani, 148
Palme, Olaf, 139
Pant, KC, 92, 105, 107
Pell, Clairborne, 18, 67
Pentagon, 74, 133-34
Percy, Charles, 67
Persian Gulf, 43-44, 107, 133
Philippines, 107

PL 480, 15, 51, 119
Plutonium products, 112
Porto Rico, 24
Portugal, 2
Powell, Jody, 32
Pressler amendment, 92
Pressler, Larry, 68
Punjab, 8, 79

Rajiv Gandhi in office, 70-85
  Assumed PM's office, 70
  Visit to US-I, 71-78
  Visit to US-II, 78-85
Rajiv-Reagan talks, 71, 74, 76
Reagan Ronald, 1, 55, 59, 67, 66, 71, 73, 74, 79, 84, 91-92, 96, 111, 116, 120, 127-28
Reagan visit to China, 62
Reddy, 32
Refuelling facilities for US aircraft during Gulf War, 6, 8, 140-42
Republican party, 79
Rogers, William, 87, 139

Saddam, 142
Sathe, Ram, 46
Saudi Arabia, 107, 142
Saxbe's, 24, 146
Schultz, George, 57, 65-66, 72
  Visit to India, 57-59
  Visit to Pakistan, 58-59
Segam, Carl, 74
Sethna, Homi, 55, 116
Shastri, Lal Bahadur, 7, 139
Sikkim, 17
Simla pact, 14, 150
Singh, VP, 107
Sino-US rapprochement, 19
Soviet action in Czechoslovakia, 18
Soviet Afghan treaty, 46
Soviet intervention by hugh influx of arms through Pakistan, 6
Soviet presence in Afghanistan, 102
Soviet troops in Afghanistan, 43, 101
Soviet troops withdrawal from Afghanistan, 92
Soviet Union, 3, 37
Sri Lanka, 105
Straits of Malacca, 132
Super Computers, 128
Swaran Singh, 2, 17, 88, 135
  Visit to Washington, 2, 17
Swedes Deep Penetration Strike Aircrafts, 100
Symington amendment, 95, 101, 109

Tamil Liberation Front, 150
Tibet, 137
Tiwari, ND, 105
Towards reconciliation, 13-27
  American attitude more rational, 13-14
  Connolly visit to New Delhi, 14
  Decision taken by US helped in restoring confidence in India, 15
  Mrs. Gandhi wrote to Nixon on Bangladesh, 13
  Process of normalisation, 14
Trishul, 106

UN Charter, 46, 141
UN General Assembly on disarmament, 36
UN Human Rights Commission, 79, 84
UN Security Council, 59
US Agency for International Development, 44

US AID, 121
US Aircraft carrier deployment in South Asia, 10
US arms supply for Pakistan, 15, 21, 48-49, 51, 58, 73, 77, 83, 87, 100, 102, 145
US Atomic Energy Commission, 112
US economic aid to India, 2, 103
US expected a change in India's foreign policy, 7
US food assistance to India, 4
US Foreign Assistance Act 1961, 95
US handing over two naval destroyers to Pakistan, 2
US imposed arms embargo in Pakistan, 87
US India agenda, 80
US lift embargo on military supplies to Pakistan, 15, 21
US military action against Libya, 84
US military build up of Pakistan, 80
US naval strategy in Indian Ocean, 132
US Nuclear Regulating Commission, 29, 112
US objective in strengthening Pakistan war machine, 92-93
US Pak relations, 20
US policy change during Afghanistan crisis, 94-95
US Senate Foreign Relation Committee, 29
US seventh Fleet in Bay of Bangal, 132
US-Soviet detente, 16
US Soviet naval race in Indian Ocean, 133
US-Soviet talks, 74
US-Soviet talks over limitation of arms race, 32
US supplied F 16 aircrafts to Pakistan, 92, 95, 101
US support to Pakistan's nuclear policy, 93
USSR, 19
US to accept on site inspection of power plants, 114
US withdrawing commitment to supply enriched uranium, 116-17

Vaidya, AS, 65
Vajpayee, Atal Behari, 30, 94, 148
Vana Cyrus, 34
Vassey, John, 67
Vassey visit to Pakistan, 67-68
Vietnam, 3, 10, 120, 138-40, 149
Vulcan Phalanse air defence equipment, 78
Vunno, 105

Watergate scandal, 16, 20, 35, 147
Weinberger, 73, 104
West German transferred technology, 94, 106
Whitehead, John G, 81
White House, 1
World Bank, 7

Yahya Khan, 87
Yoronstov, Yuri, 46

Zail Singh, 66
Zia-ul Haq, 51, 64, 78, 101
Zward, Ron, 65

US ACDA, 27

US Aircraft carrier deployment in South Asia, 16

US arms supply for Pakistan, 17, 21, 48-49, 51, 58, 75, 77, 81, 87, 100, 102, 113

US Atomic Energy Commission, 112

US economic aid to India, 2, 102

US expected a change in India's foreign policy, 7

US food assistance to India, 14

US Foreign Assistance Act 1961, 95

US handing over two naval destroyers to Pakistan, 2

US imposed arms embargo in Pakistan, 75

US-India agenda, 80

US lift embargo on military supplies to Pakistan, 15, 21

US military action against Iran, 94

US military build up of Pakistan, 20

US naval strategy in Indian Ocean, 132

US Nuclear Regulatory Commission, 29, 112

US objective of strengthening Pakistan war machine, 97-98

US Pak relations, 20

US policy change during Afghanistan crisis, 91, 95

US Senate Foreign Relation Committee, 94

US Seventh fleet in Bay of Bengal, 132

US-Soviet detente, 16

US-Soviet naval race in Indian Ocean, 133

US-Soviet talks, 79

US-Soviet talks over limitation of arms race, 22

US supplied F-16 aircraft to Pakistan, 92, 95, 101

US support to Pakistan's nuclear policies, 93

USSR, 15

US to accept on site inspection of power plants, 114

US withdrawing commitment to supply enriched uranium, 116-117

Vaidya, A.S., 65

Vajpayee, Atal Behari, 30, 64, 146

Vance, Cyrus, 34

Vassey, John, 67

Vassey visit to Pakistan, 67-68

Vietnam, 3, 10, 120, 138-40, 149

Vulcan Phalanx air defence equipment, 75

Vuono, 105

Watergate scandal, 16, 20, 35, 147

Weinberger, 73, 104

West German sophisticated technology, 94, 106

Whitehead, John C, 31

White House, 1

World Bank, 7

Yahya Khan, 87

Yorounsky, Yuri, 46

Zail Singh, 66

Zia ul Haq, 33, 64, 78, 101

Zwaard, Ron, 65